tes

"An essential guide to success in the business world. Use this book."
——*Kenneth Daly*
Midatlantic Partner in Charge
KPMG Peat Marwick LLP, Financial Services

"With this incomparable guide, your *first* five minutes can be your *best* five minutes."
——*Sheila Cluff*
President, The Oaks at Ojai/The Palms at Palm Springs
Health and Fitness Destination Spas

"This is a genuine, down-to-earth primer on how to act and look your best in business and social situations. Mary Mitchell gives you guidelines to being more successful at the office and in your personal life."
——*Dan Edelman*
Founder, Edelman Public Relations Worldwide

"Why be anything less than your best? Mary Mitchell shows you how. Invest in this book to make a great first impression."
——*Jack P. Ferguson*
Senior Vice President, Sales
Promus Hotel Corporation

"When you're in the business of doing things right, you learn to respect the work of experts such as Mary Mitchell."
——*John K. Hunter*
President, J.E. Caldwell & Co.

The First
Five Minutes

Other books by Mary Mitchell:

Dear Ms. Demeanor: The Young Person's Etiquette Guide to Handling Any Social Situation With Confidence and Grace

The Complete Idiot's Guide to Etiquette

The First Five Minutes

How to Make a Great
First Impression
in Any Business Situation

Mary Mitchell
with
John Corr

John Wiley & Sons, Inc.

New York • Chichester • Weinheim • Brisbane • Singapore • Toronto

This text is printed on acid-free paper. ♾

Copyright © 1998 by Mary Mitchell. All rights reserved.

Published by John Wiley & Sons, Inc.

Published simultaneously in Canada.

This publication is designed to provide accurate and authoritative information in regard to the subject matter covered. It is sold with the understanding that the publisher is not engaged in rendering professional services. If legal, accounting, medical, psychological, or any other expert assistance is required, the services of a competent professional person should be sought.

Library of Congress Cataloging-in-Publication Data
Mitchell, Mary
    The first five minutes : how to make a great first impression in
any business situation / Mary Mitchell with John Corr.
        p.   cm.
    Includes index.
    ISBN 0-471-18478-0 (pbk. : alk. paper)
    1. Career development.   2. Social interaction.   3. Self
-presentation.   4. Success in business.   I. Corr, John, 1934–
II. Title.
HF5381.M58   1998
650.1—dc21   97–37395

Printed in the United States of America

10 9 8 7 6 5 4 3 2 1

For my mom

Preface

First impressions often are as shallow as rain water on a leaky roof.

Yet they are about as permanent as concrete, and if you're like most people, it would take at least a crowbar or an act of God to change them.

Is this fair? Certainly not. Perceptions are neither fair nor unfair. They are simply perceptions and they exist. They are important. They can make or break a budding relationship. And although we live in an age of technology, we cannot afford to forget that our relationships form the foundation of our work life.

The fact is that receiving a first impression is an uncomplicated experience. On the other hand, giving a first impression, a positive first impression, can be anything but. It's fair to say that awareness is the key, and that's why I wrote this book.

The overall impression I received from the people I worked with in my corporate training was that we present ourselves in business with altogether too little fore-thought and preparation. Chiefly, individuals only consider face-to-face meetings when they think about first impressions. That limited view cheats us of some invaluable information.

We all have the right to present ourselves as best we can. We all have the right to the best job and best work for which we're qualified.

This book is my best effort to provide significant help along the way.

Acknowledgments

Writing a book while your mother is dying is an almost impossible task.

If it were not for the considerable assistance of my colleague and friend John Corr, this book would not exist. Perhaps his finest contribution was never letting me settle for less than my best work. Marjorie Matthews Corr, his wife and also my friend, graciously became our unofficial editor. I am grateful and proud to share my life and work with them.

Nor would this book exist without Nancy Love, my agent, and PJ Dempsey, former Wiley editor, who together came up with the idea for it in the first place. Judith McCarthy at Wiley shepherded it through to conclusion with care and insight.

John Hunter, president of J.E. Caldwell & Company in Philadelphia, generously provided his company's splendid resources in the persons of Janet Weiss, manager of Caldwell's remarkable stationery department, and her aide de camp Sarah Packer. They willingly shared their extraordinary depth of knowledge as well as provided all the examples in this book.

Letitia Baldrige's work and career have been the most profound influence on my own. She believes, as I do, that warmth and kindness are the soul of etiquette. Having her as friend and mentor is a great blessing.

Because this book is largely based on the corporate training that is the cornerstone of my work, while functioning as teacher, I have learned much from my clients. Thea Lammers brought a sense of creative, practical excellence that characterized those programs.

The Reverends John and Betsy Salunek helped keep me close to God when my faith was indeed challenged.

Each and every day, Dan Fleischmann, my best friend who happens to be my husband, inspires me to be the finest person I can be. Throughout the sad and painful time when this book was in progress, his mere presence constantly reminded me what a privilege it is to give of one's time and talent. He made me laugh, see things differently, and remain curious. As long as he continues to do that, I shall keep on writing.

Introduction

Your mother was right—you never get a second chance to make a first impression.

The moment you walk into a room, you communicate dozens of nuggets of information that people instantly pick up and use to begin forming an opinion of who you are. It all happens quickly, and it's pretty much a done deal by the time the first few minutes have elapsed.

And once that opinion—good or bad, right or wrong—has been formed, it is difficult, if not impossible, for you to change it. You know that this is the way people respond when meeting someone new because you do it yourself.

It's not only dress and posture and grooming that send signals, although these are vitally important; it's also that indefinable look of someone who is ready, confident, and relaxed; someone you feel you will enjoy meeting, knowing, and working with; someone, perhaps, with leadership potential.

We say people like this have a natural ability to make a good impression and to get along well with others. We say they have a natural gift for putting people at ease.

Well, those people were not born that way. Nobody is. The techniques, skills, and attitudes that allow us to present

---

ourselves in an effective, positive way are not instinctive. We have to learn them, and the more we learn, the better presentation we will make.

Part of my own education in this area came to me as a corporate wife, living abroad and doing a great deal of entertaining in international diplomatic, banking, and business circles. Another part came in the next 15 years, which I spent in marketing, as founder and president of the Mitchell Organization. During this period, I was asked often to speak to corporate executives about effective communication, appearance, and people skills. This led to my formation of Uncommon Courtesies, a company that trains employees at all levels in social skills and that also arranges business and social functions in the United States and abroad for multinational corporations.

All of these experiences have taught me over and over again the critical importance of first impressions and have brought home to me the fact that so many otherwise capable and intelligent people lack basic techniques and insights that could help them enormously in this area. That's what this book is all about. It's about how we communicate, how we look and sound, and how we present ourselves in various situations—business and social, formal, casual, or critical. It presents in an orderly and easy-to-understand way the information and skills that will make those you meet respond positively to you, and at the same time give you the confidence and bearing that mark you immediately as one of those people with a natural gift for making that crucial first impression favorable.

1

First Impressions

The first time you meet someone, you step into a bright and unforgiving circle of light. Everything about you is intensified and exaggerated—your manner, gestures, voice, and facial expressions. And you may not just passively submit to examination. You must "present yourself."

This book is about being at ease and letting yourself shine in this circle of light. It is essentially a book for people in business, but it aims to provide specific, accessible information to everyone about how to avoid disaster and how to create a favorable first impression in any business or social situation. This information includes rules, techniques, and tips on such things as introductions and greetings—both casual and formal—grooming and dress, office visits and visitors, electronic etiquette, making conversation, and posture and body language.

It is also about presenting yourself in the best light in situations that could prove to be difficult, sensitive, or complicated. For example:

- Job interviews
- Business meals, dinner parties, and other occasions involving food
- Responding to conflict, criticism, and compliments
- Dealing with ethnic and cultural diversity
- Meeting and working with the disabled

Danger and Opportunity

Whether you are walking into someone's office, being introduced at a cocktail party, or meeting people while wearing a hard hat on a job site, first encounters are fraught with social dangers as well as opportunities. You could be guilty of any one of a long list of unintentional goofs, little irritations, and/or distractions. Your attire and posture could be sending the wrong message. Worse, you may appear to be anxious, uncomfortable, or lacking in poise, when what you want most of all is to appear to be at ease.

When you are at ease, it puts others at ease and makes them more disposed to respond positively to you. But "ease" is not easy. The only way to get there is through careful preparation and attention to detail.

One of the first things dealt with in this book, in Chapter 2, "Communication Styles," is the different ways in which different people receive information and how you can quickly spot the signals that will help you to decide how to present yourself and your message.

The rules and techniques for greeting people in varying situations and circumstances must become so familiar that they come into play almost automatically. There is a right way and a wrong way to make introductions and to introduce yourself. There are techniques for shaking hands and making eye contact. These and more are covered in Chapter 3, "Tried-and-True Greeting Strategies."

Nothing sends out a more immediate first-impression message than dress and grooming. Chapters 4 and 5 make the point that there is no such thing as neutral clothing and no compromising when it comes to grooming. Big decisions have to be made about what you wear and how you look, and these chapters provide guidelines, theory, and practical tips.

Chapters 6 and 7 deal with how you look and how you act during job interviews and at business meetings. Not only making a right first impression, but doing it over and over again and in changing situations and relationships, is the subject of Chapter 8.

As soon as you meet someone, you must be ready to engage in conversation. In Chapter 9, you will find that there is nothing small about small talk. Chapter 10 deals with talking to groups; it lays out ways to overcome dread of public speaking and to use the occasion to make a dynamite first impression.

Often people create their first impression through written correspondence or electronic communication, whether it be by telephone or by computer. These are covered in Chapters 11 and 12.

You are never more "on stage" than when you are delivering or receiving compliments or criticism or when you are dealing with conflict situations. All of this is dealt with in Chapter 13.

Many first impressions occur across the dining table or in other situations involving food. What to expect and how to behave at everything from a black-tie dinner to a burger at Mickey D's are covered in Chapter 14.

In this constantly shrinking world, you are more likely than ever to be meeting and impressing people from other cultures and other parts of the world. Handling these encounters smoothly and knowledgeably is the topic of Chapter 15.

Finally, Chapter 16 deals with taking the tension out of meeting, greeting, and dealing with those with disabilities.

One Good and One Bad Encounter

Throughout the book, first encounters are presented in the form of scenarios that portray meetings between different characters—bosses and subordinates, Asians and Westerners, the disabled and the able-bodied—and in various situations—business meetings, job interviews, and luncheons. These scenarios illustrate the successes and disasters that can happen in the first few minutes of any meeting and the reasons for each.

The Bad

As an example, let's follow junior executive Tom Conway as he arrives for a 9 A.M. meeting with Carter Fitzpatrick, CEO (chief executive officer) of Cobalt Manufacturing. Conway has been named as liaison between Cobalt and his company, Telefont, and he figures to be spending a lot of time at Cobalt over the coming six months. He secretly hopes that his assignment will lead ultimately to his being hired for a top position at Cobalt. On this rainy November Monday, he is having his first meeting with Fitzpatrick.

Conway arrives at the receptionist's desk at 9:01 A.M., wet and out of breath. "Hi, honey. Is Fitzpatrick in? We have a meet."

The receptionist gives Conway a frosty look and says, "Mr. Fitzpatrick is expecting you. This way, please."

Fitzpatrick comes around the desk to greet Conway as he enters the office, umbrella in one hand, briefcase in the other. Fitzpatrick calls the receptionist back and asks her to take the umbrella and the dripping raincoat. Conway notices that Fitzpatrick is dressed much more formally than he is.

Then, the men shake hands, and Conway remarks, "I had a hell of a time finding a place to park."

Fitzpatrick informs him, "We have a private lot behind the building."

"Oh. I didn't know."

Conway pulls a chair to the side of Fitzpatrick's desk, sits down, and begins taking papers out of his briefcase.

"Anyway, nice to meet you, Carter," he says. "Looks like we'll be working together quite a bit. I have some ideas about organizing and coordinating production schedules."

Carter Fitzpatrick pauses, appears to make up his mind about something, and says, "Well, I expect you will be dealing mainly with our Ms. McCarthy. In fact, I'll call her in now, and you two can get started."

Conway has squandered an irreplaceable opportunity to make a winning first impression. Worse, he has created a negative impression that will be difficult, if not impossible, to erase. (I always say it takes a crowbar to pry *me* loose from my first impressions.)

The Good

And his mistakes could so easily have been avoided and the negatives turned into positives. Here's how those first five minutes could have gone with the proper planning and preparation:

Conway arrives at 8:50 A.M. Through an earlier "scouting" visit, he learned, among other things:

1. Where to park
2. The company dress code
3. The receptionist's name

"Good morning, Mrs. Goddard. I'm Tom Conway from Telefont. I have a 9 o'clock appointment with Mr. Fitzpatrick. Is there somewhere I can put my coat and umbrella?"

He enters Fitzpatrick's office unencumbered and smiling. He greets the other man with a handshake and eye contact, says, "Good morning, Mr. Fitzpatrick" (not "Carter"), and waits to be told where to sit.

He also waits for Fitzpatrick to take the conversational lead.

"How was your trip?" Fitzpatrick asks.

"Fine," replies Conway, "except for all of this rain."

They chat a moment about the weather. Conway waits for the other man to get to the business of the meeting and calls him "Mr. Fitzpatrick" until the other man says, "Call me Carter."

Life and human behavior are not as neatly categorized, of course, as in our two little scenarios, and most of us are confident that we would not make the same mistakes that Tom Conway did while shooting himself in both feet during the crucial first few minutes of his meeting.

But without proper preparation, thought, and planning, many of us would make some of those blunders or others just as damaging to our goal of cashing in on that one-time-only opportunity to make a favorable first impression.

2

Communication Styles

The first five minutes of my first job interview convinced me that I had no chance of getting the job. The interviewer came out of his office to meet me. His jacket was off, his tie was askew, and his manner was curt.

"Miss Mitchell?"

I stood up.

"Follow me."

I obeyed.

In his office, he sat behind his desk and said, "Sit down."

I sat.

"Why do you think you should have this job?"

Although dismayed, I carried on as well as I could, and the interview ended as brusquely as it had begun. I wrote off the possibility of getting the job and went on to other things.

The interviewer and I met socially a few years later, and the subject of the interview arose. I told him my reaction to the interview.

"That's too bad," he said. "You were a prime candidate."

It occurred to me that my life might have taken a different turn if the interviewer had been able to communicate that. In fact, his appearance, manner, and speech communicated just the opposite.

It's been proven over and over that what we say is not necessarily what people hear. Studies on the overall impression that people make in the first few minutes when they meet show that 7 percent of that impression is based on what a person says, 38 percent on how he or she says it, and 55 percent on what the other person SEES. We are, after all, visual creatures, no matter how verbal we think we are.

When we first meet a person, that person is taking in an entire picture of us, and what we are saying at the moment is only a part of the picture. Communication at that moment is not just about what we are saying, but also about what others *think* we are saying. Their perception is more important than our intention, and their perception controls how they will react to us and judge us.

So, what they hear is more important than what we say. And because the same word can mean different things to different people, a lot depends on nonverbal communication, which includes our appearance, our mannerisms, and our body language.

Minding the Body

Dress and grooming, of course, are critical elements that affect how people respond to us, but so is body language. Communication is facilitated by an open appearance. Crossing your arms in front of you, for example, "closes" the body and creates a barrier between you and the other person. (Women tend to cross their arms more than men and have to work harder to break the habit.)

Other important aspects of body language are posture and gestures. Negative messages go out from people who slouch, study their shoes, or sit or walk rigidly. Gestures such as twirling hair, jabbing with fingers, or clenching fists can communicate all of the wrong messages.

And getting involved in space wars also hinders easy and effective communications, particularly during first encounters with strangers. Americans are generally most comfortable speaking at about an arm's length from one another. If you are too far away or, especially, if you are crowding the other person, you are creating a discomfort level that interferes with communication.

Space frontiers may vary, however. If you are speaking and the listener moves a little closer, don't back off unless you find the proximity distinctly disturbing. Conversely, if the listener backs off a bit, resist the impulse to pursue. He's likely doing it because you are too close.

"Sound" Techniques

The first time someone hears you speak, he or she will have a tendency to associate certain personality traits with the way you sound. For example, a resonant baritone may convey dependability, whereas a flat, weak voice conveys blandness. If your first conversation is by telephone, the other person may go even further and associate physical characteristics with your vocal characteristics.

Listen to your voice. Chances are you are still using your "child" voice, the vocal patterns you learned growing up.

Listen for and try to change nasal tones, thinness, raspy sounds, and other unattractive elements. Work to develop resonance without booming like a camp meeting revivalist.

Tape yourself, preferably during a conversation. You may find the results sobering. You may want to invest in voice classes or acting classes that stress vocal development.

However, no amount of vocal acuity will replace sincerity. Imagine that you are at the theater, and the plot takes a tragic turn. You think you should be feeling something, but you aren't. The reason could be that the actors are not "feeling something."

Have you ever asked yourself: "How can I successfully sell a product (or an idea) in which I don't believe?" The answer is: You can't, no matter how good an actor you think you are. If you want to be a convincing advocate of a product or an idea, you must find something about it that you support and believe in. Once you have convinced yourself, you can go about the task of convincing others with confidence and authority.

Tuning In to Personality Types

During those first moments of any new encounter, while the other person is forming judgments about you, you should be looking for clues as to the best way to convey the message you want to send to him or her.

There are three major factors that affect the way people receive and process information—personality type, learning style, and gender. You don't have to be a clinical psychologist to understand and deal with the dynamics involved in these three factors.

When meeting with someone with whom I will be doing business, I try to discern as quickly as I can the type of personality with which I will be dealing. It helps one to divide personality types into four categories—activist, controller, consensus seeker, and logician—and to look for insights as to where people fit. If we can recognize the group into which an individual falls, we will be more effective in communicating with him or her.

As we become more sophisticated, we tend to have qualities from all of the groups, but one or two of these will always be our most dominant characteristics. None of these four types is good or bad, better or worse. They are just different.

In each of these groups, we are going to look for the person's "unwritten rule," the prime motivator.

The Activist

For the activist, the prime motivator is to be appreciated. If you or someone else in your life is an activist, you and they thrive on appreciation and, of course, action.

The activist wants his information in terms of the big picture. Details tend to make his eyes glaze over. Also, people are very important to him. He absorbs information quickly and tends to make decisions spontaneously, based on enthusiasm and gut responses. He works well as part of a team because of his people orientation.

A clue that you are dealing with an activist might be a messy work environment because, for one reason, he is not detail-oriented. He is interested not only in being appreciated but in having a good time. He is the type who will attend a seminar and write down all the jokes so that he can repeat them the next day at the office.

13

The Controller

The unwritten rule, the prime motivator for the controller is, "Let's do it! Let's get it done!"

She wants her information promptly and completely. Because she is results-driven, time is important and wasting time is not only annoying, but sinful. If you want to see the controller's eyes light up, uses phrases such as "Let's cut to the chase" or "Let's get to the bottom line."

Because the controller likes challenge and risk, she will also respond positively to such phrases as "This could be a risky proposition" and "It's a big challenge for us."

Like the activist, the controller makes decisions quickly. She likes action, control, and results.

The Consensus Seeker

The prime motivator for the consensus seeker is, "Let's get along." This person is extremely people-oriented and works well with a team. He wants a lot of information and a number of points of view. He will not make a quick decision, and when he does, the decision will reflect the feelings and positions of those with whom he is working.

The consensus seeker wants to be sure that everyone understands, that everyone is comfortable. He is introspective and conscientious, loyal, appreciative, and caring. A clue that you are dealing with such a personality is that the working environment will be orderly and, as far as possible, peaceful. The consensus seeker functions poorly, if at all, amid chaos.

The Logician

The unwritten rule for the logician is, "Get it right." The logician wants information in great detail and in writing.

Given a choice between 2 pages and 106, she'll take the 106. And the logician is happiest with hard information—numbers and twice-proven data. Also, she works best and is happiest working alone.

The logician makes decisions slowly and with caution. If you need a timely decision, try to bypass the logician in favor of the activist or the controller.

I was discussing the logician at a seminar once and one woman acknowledged having logician tendencies, saying she alphabetized her spice rack.

"Not only that," a man in the front offered, "I alphabetize my soup cans."

Someone in the back blurted out, "What a wonderful idea!"

We may not be able to spot enough clues in the first few minutes in the company of a stranger to fix firmly on that individual's personality type. But by thinking in terms of these four categories, we are more apt to pick up clues that can help us to communicate more effectively even at the beginning of a relationship.

Looking at Learning Styles

Another helpful tool in deciding on the best means of communicating with someone you have just met is to look for signs that reflect that person's learning style, which means how he or she receives information. You can pick up hints to a person's learning style by watching their reaction to how new information is presented.

Let's say three people buy the same VCR. The first reads the instruction manual from beginning to end before even taking the VCR out of the box. This one can be called a VISUAL learner. The second person gets the VCR unpacked and calls a friend for advice on how to make it operational. This one is an AUDITORY learner. The third hooks it up and begins to work buttons until he's got it working to his satisfaction. He or she is a TACTILE learner.

Suppose you have an idea you want to sell to a new client. If the person is the *visual* type, you might be most successful by writing it out and, perhaps, including graphics: "I have worked out a plan for coordinating your telecommunications systems. Here's a description of the idea and a couple of rough graphs. Look it over and let me know what you think."

If the client is *auditory*, the best approach might be to call or to set up a meeting and just talk about the idea: "I've been thinking about a way of coordinating telecommunications. We can start by bringing together . . ."

If *tactile*, you would look for a way to demonstrate the idea or to have the person experience it in some way: "I can show you how a console at key locations can bring together your telecommunications systems and give your people easier access."

He Said, She Said

There are, of course, other factors affecting learning styles. An important one is gender.

In terms of equal treatment and equal respect, it doesn't matter if the person you have just met is a man or a woman. In terms of communications during those first few crucial minutes, it could matter a great deal.

For example, studies have shown that when men nod their heads, they most often are saying "I agree." However, when women nod their heads, they are most often saying, "Yes, I follow you. Keep going." *Don't assume that a nod means approval.*

Also, men tend to be more comfortable talking side to side, whereas women are most comfortable talking face to face. So if a woman is speaking with a man, she should not be put off by the fact that he has a tendency to move out of a face-to-face situation. And men should be aware that women may feel more comfortable conversing head-on. Women may find it particularly annoying when men choose to bring up important matters in the car, where side-by-side conversation is unavoidable. I understand now why my husband always launches into an important discussion while we are driving to a restaurant, whereas I usually wait until we have arrived and are sitting across from each other.

Women tend to color their narratives with details, whereas men tend to hurry to the conclusion. A woman might begin by saying, "The meeting was held in the large, windowless ballroom, and the hard plastic chairs were very uncomfortable. These factors may account for the fact that so little was accomplished."

The man's version might begin, "The only thing settled at the meeting was the agenda for tomorrow. It might have been that the venue was wrong."

So, a man may become impatient and may be tempted to interrupt a woman's narrative. She can avoid this by starting with the outcome and filling in the details later.

Men, on the other hand, tend to "tell" rather than "discuss." Their voices may rise and their body language may become intrusive from a woman's perspective when they are trying to make a point. They are likely to say, "Hand me that Greenleaf report," rather than, "Would you please pass that report to me?"

And men and women generally have different ways of bonding, or solidifying relationships. Men love to advise each other about the best way to find, accomplish, or get rid of something. They use humor and sarcasm and even mild insults. They talk about external things, particularly sports.

Women form bonds by sharing personal information and by complimenting each other. They tend to be disappointed when men refuse to talk about their feelings. Men tend to bolt or clam up when women try to get them to open up.

This, of course, means that communicating with the opposite sex can require effort and change on your part. But a good communicator is someone who is willing to change, who accepts all of the responsibility for effective communication.

And effective communication is less about the message we send than about the message the other person receives. This has been true since Org and Og met in some primeval forest and tried to decide whether to bash each other, grunt affably, or ignore one another.

3

Tried-and-True
Greeting Strategies

Pam Thompson is being introduced to people at the Telefont head office as a personnel consultant. Only she and the CEO (chief executive officer) know that after an orientation period, she will become the vice president for human resources.

She comes into Greg Jones's office with sales executive Rob Foster. Rob says, "Pam, I'd like you to meet Greg Jones. Greg is our regional sales manager."

Rob turns to Jones and adds, "Pam will be consulting with us for the next several weeks."

Jones leans forward in his chair, extends his hand across his desk, and says, "Hi, Pam. Welcome to the madhouse."

Thompson takes his hand but does not smile. She is thinking, "This guy should have 'amateur' stamped on his forehead."

Basic Training

Jones thinks he is being natural and friendly, a "nice-to-meet-ya" kind of guy. Actually, he is being insulting and is creating a first impression that will be difficult if not impossible to erase.

In every situation, there is a lot more going on at the moment of meeting than simply making an acquaintance. Whether or not we are conscious of it, our emotions are involved.

There is something that all of us want from each other and from the world. It is simple acknowledgment. We want people to recognize our presence, to thank us for favors, to praise our best efforts, and to respond in kind to our communications.

And we want to be greeted politely. There is more to a simple, proper greeting than meets the eye, and it comes in many forms:

- We greet people we know or people we have never met before.
- We shake hands, or we don't.
- We greet others one-on-one or when they (or we) are part of a group.
- We are introduced, or we introduce others.

Whatever the situation, there are certain basics that apply to every situation. For example, if you are seated, stand up. Always rise to the occasion when greeting someone and usually when someone new comes on the scene. There was a time when women remained seated when new people arrived. Those days are over. However, when newcomers arrive at a very large function, only those nearest them rise to greet them. And if it would be clumsy or inconvenient for you to rise—you may be wedged behind a restaurant table—lean forward or rise just slightly so you don't appear aloof.

If Pam Thompson were brought to your office, the right thing to do would be to stand and come around the desk to greet her. (See the section on visiting in Chapter 8.) This is how you must greet all visitors to your office, unless they are co-workers or someone else who visits frequently. (The frequency consideration is valid even when a senior executive visits the office of a junior executive. The junior executive will, however, stop whatever he is doing and give his full attention to the senior, if he has any sense.)

Someone will then make the introduction. (See "Introductions: The Rules" later in this chapter.) Look at the introducer as he speaks, then at the newcomer.

Make eye contact, smile, put out your hand, and say, "Hello Ms. Thompson," followed by "It's a pleasure to meet you" or "Welcome to Telefont."

It will continue to be "Ms. Thompson" until, if ever, she says, "Call me Pam."

You can say something like "I've been looking forward to meeting you" or "I've heard a lot about you," but only if it's true and if what you have heard is good. Remember that sincerity is the key.

Ms. (pronounced "mizz") is the correct way to address women in the workplace, regardless of what she chooses to call herself in her private life. *Mrs.* and *Miss* imply social, marital, and sexual distinctions that have no place in business. Of course, if a woman asks you to call her "Mrs." or

"Miss," it is best to comply. Then, if you are introducing her as "Mrs.," you use her given first name—Mrs. *Sally* Jones, not Mrs. Henry Jones. (See "Introductions: The Rules.")

Whole Lotta Shakin'

Shaking hands is the only really appropriate physical contact for both men and women in the business world. It is an extremely important part of making a good first impression.

And speaking of first, the person who extends his hand first has an advantage. Being first gives you a measure of control, and business is all about control. So, always be ready to shake hands. That means remembering to leave your right hand free of food, drinks, files, and so on.

At business functions or social gatherings, check any bags and carry only a small shoulder bag. If you suffer from clammy hands, you might want to spray them with an antiperspirant. It generally takes twenty-four hours for antiperspirants to kick in, so you might want to spray your hands daily if clammy hands are a chronic problem. Don't put any fragrance on your hands. I once caused a client a sneezing attack because he was allergic to a hand lotion fragrance I was wearing.

For your own comfort and protection, don't wear rings on your right hand. They could get squeezed into your skin in a hearty handshake.

How and When to Shake

Always extend your hand open, and make sure your feet are planted firmly so that you don't rock.

Try to get your hand all the way into the other person's hand so that the web between your thumb and index finger makes contact, locking thumb to thumb. This is the best way to avoid giving or receiving either a "bone crusher" or a "limp fish" handshake. Both are bad news in the business arena, as is the two-hand clasp. They convey volumes of negative information about the people employing them.

The bone crusher usually is an extremely insecure yet aggressive person. Men are more apt to do this than women. The limp fish handshake says the person is ambivalent about his or her role in a given situation. It can also give the impression that the person doesn't really care or even that he or she finds shaking hands distasteful. The two-handed clasp is fine if you are a minister consoling someone. In a way, it is even more aggressive than the bone crusher shake, and it certainly has no place in the business world. People use the two-hand clasp because they think it communicates sincerity. My instant reaction always is, "You protest too much."

Make eye contact. You can bend forward slightly, but don't rock. Don't pump more than a couple of times. Don't let the handshake last more than three seconds, and never try to continue a shake for the duration of an introduction. It can begin to feel and look like a Marx Brothers routine.

I've noticed that women often come in too close when shaking a taller man's hand. This causes them to rock backward during the handshake, giving the impression that the woman's power and authority have diminished.

Handshakes are appropriate not only when meeting someone but whenever someone offers his or her hand to you—when you are saying goodbye and when you are meeting or parting from your host or your guests at a social function.

Touching Situations

Touching others, even those of the same gender, is generally inappropriate in the workplace, even if the other person is your pal, or you think he or she is. This includes draping your arm on someone's shoulder or patting someone on the back. Hugs and kisses are out of the question. It is acceptable at a business/social function, however, to give your spouse a short welcoming kiss, if you happen to be getting along that day.

Introductions: The Rules

Making introductions is one area of business and social life where you have to know the rules. Knowing the introduction rules will put you at ease, and this will come across to those you are introducing, putting them at ease as well.

Who's on First

Precedence is paramount when it comes to introductions. The rule is: *The person of greater authority or importance is mentioned first.* For example, "Mr./Ms. Chairman, I would like to introduce Mr./Ms. Junior Executive."

Social etiquette is based on the old rules of chivalry, so in a social situation we may defer to people based on age or gender. Business etiquette, however, is based on rank and authority. Gender plays no role.

There is, however, an exception to the "greater authority-lesser authority" rule. The president of your company is not more important than your client: "Mr. Cassidy, I would like to introduce Ms. Grimsley, our chief executive officer.

Mr. Cassidy is our client from London." An alternative is to use full names for both, dropping the honorifics. "John Cassidy, I would like to introduce Paula Grimsley, our chief executive officer."

When introducing peers, it doesn't matter who is mentioned first. It is gracious, harking back to chivalric system of social etiquette.

The "who's first" rule is not the only one governing introductions. When you are making an introduction, look at each person in turn. First, look at and speak to the person of greater authority, and then look at and speak to the person of lesser authority.

Adding Valuable Nuggets

Always supply more than the name alone. Supplying a nugget of information about the people being introduced helps both of them feel more comfortable with each other and provides a basis for beginning a conversation. It can also serve as a warning. For example, you could be letting someone know that they are being introduced to a member of the media and might be speaking "on the record."

A typical nugget might be "Mr. Cassidy has just arrived from Tucson" or "Mr. Cassidy's field is personnel management."

You don't need to add that Cassidy is staying at the Hilton or is here with his wife and grandson. When in doubt, less personal is better than more personal.

But THE most important thing about introductions is to *make them.* If you don't make introductions because you are hesitant about how to proceed, the people around you will become quite uncomfortable. It is better to take a chance on botching things than to do nothing.

Introducing Yourself

Never be shy about introducing yourself, even when you might have been introduced previously. In many situations, it is absolutely necessary. You introduce yourself when:

- You are at a gathering and don't know the others.
- When someone seems to remember you, but is unable to place you. Say something like, "We met at the Flower Show last year. I remember you were particularly interested in the Japanese gardens."
- When you are seated next to someone at a meal.
- When the person expected to make the introductions fails to do so.

At a gathering, just smile and extend your hand to the nearest person: "Hello, I'm Ellen Copley. Tom Franks and I are working on the Comtech project."

Mentioning what you are doing rather than just a title is friendly and more apt to promote conversation. However, don't pile on details. It is not necessary to mention right off how long you have been with the company or that you had trouble finding a place to park. For example, "I'm Mary Mitchell. I have worked for companies throughout the country training employees in social skills" is better than "I'm Mary Mitchell, president of Uncommon Courtesies."

Responding to Introductions

Knowing how to respond when you are being introduced is just as important as knowing how to make introductions. If it is an informal introduction, you simply say, "Hello, Mr. Allen." A simple "Hi" or "Hello" is not enough. Use the person's name, and perhaps add a small comment: "I enjoyed reading your paper on cell phone cloning." If you do add a comment, keep it brief and friendly.

If it is a formal introduction, say, "How do you do," followed by the person's name. Formal or informal, don't use the person's first name until invited to do so.

Remember that "How do you do" is not a literal question. The proper response to "How do you do" is "How do you do."

Never give yourself an honorific. Introduce yourself by your first and last name. If you have a professional title, you can say, "I'm Lillian Mitchell. I'm a dentist from Philadelphia." This gives the other person the cue to say, "Hello, Dr. Mitchell."

Business/Social Functions

There are other considerations that come into play when it comes to meeting, greeting, and introducing people at business/social functions.

The host should meet and greet the guests and make them feel welcome. If this is not possible or if the host doesn't know the guests by name, he may designate a replacement greeter or have someone more knowledgeable join him in receiving the guests.

If there is a substitute greeter, he introduces himself and escorts the guest to the host. After the greeter makes the introductions, he should move the guest along, introducing him to others or taking him to the buffet table or the bar so that the host will be free to receive other guests.

The substitute greeter begins with a handshake, saying, "Hello, I'm Troy Gallagher. Thanks for coming."

After he gets the visitor's name, Troy says, "Come along and meet our president, Jean Powell." At social functions, first and last names are generally appropriate.

Then: "Jean Powell, this is Henry Carver, the architect on the Greenleaf project."

And finally: "Mr. Carver, you might want to chat with Joan Jakes, who just came in from Tucson to help us with some consulting work" or "The bar and the buffet are just over this way."

It is not necessary to introduce a newcomer to everyone at a social function. Introduce him to the closest person or group, saying his name first and then naming the others in the group or asking the group members to introduce themselves.

Names and Titles

Again, we are all sensitive about being acknowledged. Names and titles are crucial, and getting them right is crucial to making a good first impression.

Rankings

In the business world, because rank is of utmost importance and titles signify rank, getting the title right is almost as important as getting the name right. For example, you cannot refer to the chief operating officer as the chief executive officer or to the senior vice president as the vice president or to an administrative assistant as a secretary.

No matter what you call the boss in private, when you are with others—particularly those from outside the company— you address him or her as Mr. or Ms. Smith and refer to him or her in the same way.

Saying It Right

Even the most forgiving souls wince inwardly when you mispronounce their names. When in doubt about pronunciation, ask. You can say, "I'm sorry, but I'm not sure I know how to pronounce your name correctly. Can you help me out?"

If someone is introduced to you and you miss the name, ask apologetically, but immediately, for the name to be repeated.

Never, ever try to make a joke about a person's name, even if the person is not present. These jokes are not funny and have a way of getting back to the party being ridiculed.

If your name is difficult to pronounce, it is a gracious gesture to help out someone who is trying to pronounce it correctly and botching the job. You can smile and say something like, "It's a tough one, isn't it?" And pronounce the name clearly, making as little of it as possible. Your gesture will be appreciated and remembered.

The Dead Zone

Yes, all of us have had the experience of coming up blank where a name is concerned. Don't let that stop you, and don't make a big deal out of it. You can say, "Please tell me your name again. I'm having a memory gridlock right now." This is my favorite approach because it focuses on the solution instead of the problem.

If you remember the circumstances under which you met the person previously, you can say, "I remember our conversation after the management seminar, but I've forgotten your name for the moment." Get the name, and go right ahead with the introduction. Apologies are not necessary and will only draw attention to the uncomfortable situation. Everyone has experienced what I call "mental vapor lock" and will not be inclined to judge you harshly.

When you are meeting people and want to remember their names, a good trick is to say the name to yourself immediately and repeat it as soon as you can during the conversation.

If you are meeting someone you know slightly, and you suspect that he or she has forgotten your name, immediately put out your hand, smile, and say your name.

Business Cards

Because greeting people in the business world often involves the exchange of business cards, it is important to remember that the business card is so much more than a piece of paper with words and numbers on it. It is an important part of your personal presence.

What and How

You must know how to present your card and what the card itself should look like.

There are three principal uses for business cards:

1. To convey vital information about you—your name, your company, your title, and the phone/fax number(s) at which you can be reached.
2. To append to a document, photograph, or other material you want to circulate.
3. To enclose with a gift or flowers.

When giving your card, present it with the type side up. When someone hands you a card, look at it and then at the giver so you can connect the name with the face, and then put it away.

Avoid Papering the House

When do you give your business card, and to whom do you give it? Don't thrust your card on anyone, particularly a senior executive. Wait until you are asked for it.

If you are in a group, don't pass your cards out to everyone there. It's pushy and gives the impression that you are trying to sell something. Giving your card to everyone and anyone who will take it is a bad idea, in general, and you may regret supplying a stranger with your name, business address, and telephone number.

Be unobtrusive about giving someone your card at a social function. Think of it as a private exchange between two individuals. And your card should never surface during a meal, whether it's at Burger King or the Ritz Carlton. You should have your cards with you because you never know when someone will ask for one, but don't produce one without being asked specifically. On the other hand, if there is someone who has not asked for your card and you want to be sure that he or she has it, ask, "May I give you my card?" (not "Here's my card").

If your cards are soiled, damaged, or out of date, dump them and get new ones. If you don't have cards in good condition, apologize and write out the information on a clean piece of paper.

Your Greeting Style

While it is important to remember the rules and helpful hints in this chapter, it is even more important to think about the style of your greeting, which can be far more important than its form. The style should be friendly, open, and generous.

No greeting should be so formal that it is without warmth. When you are preparing to meet someone, tell yourself that this is a person whom you will enjoy meeting and who might even end up being a friend. If you do that, your smile will be returned, and there will be a ring of truth in your voice when you say, "I'm glad to meet you."

4

Clothing and Accessories

"We have a busy day scheduled for you tomorrow, Tom. You'll be attending your first board meeting in the morning, and I'll be introducing you to the engineer and the architect in the afternoon at the new construction site."

On hearing this, Tom should immediately be aware of two things. First, he must be ready tomorrow to make a strong first impression on a number of people, and second, he will have to make time at midday to change his clothes.

The judgments that people make about us in the first moments after we meet them are more strongly influenced by how we look than by anything else. And how we look is intrinsically joined with how we dress.

Wearing the same clothing to the board meeting as to the construction site would be tantamount to wearing work boots to the ballet. Where we are and what we are doing dictates to a large degree what we wear in the business world, and we must fashion our fashion statement to suit the circumstances. Different cloaks for different folks.

There Is No Such Thing as Neutral Clothing

Everything you put on represents a decision you have made and is a reflection of your good taste, your good sense, and your style. The first time people see you, they will react instantly to the way you are dressed, whether they realize it or not.

Socially, they may make a snap decision about your social status or about whether you would be an interesting or agreeable person to know.

Professionally, their reaction can be even more harshly judgmental. If your attire is inappropriate, colleagues are apt to question whether you know the rules of the game and whether you are or are not likely to be a significant player. Your superiors are apt to conclude that the quality of your work will match the quality of your appearance.

Dressing for the Situation

There is an unspoken prejudice against those who do not follow the rules of etiquette in general and dress in particular. And a standard "dress for success" uniform is no guarantee. Successful people dress appropriately for specific occasions and situations.

When you are considering how to dress to make the most impressive first impression for a certain occasion or situation, it is helpful to ask yourself some questions:

- Who am I, and how do I want to be perceived?
- Where am I, and who are the people I want to impress favorably?

A friend of mine related the story of her son's first job interview. After graduating with a degree from the University of Pennsylvania's prestigious Wharton School of Business, he applied at a Wall Street financial institution wearing an expensive navy blue suit, a custom-made shirt, an alligator belt, Gucci shoes, and a "tweety-bird" necktie and braces. His mom thought the outfit was a delightful statement of his personality. Maybe so. But he didn't get the job.

On the other hand, a person might show up at an interview for a writer's job at an ad agency wearing a gray Brooks Brothers suit, a blue oxford cloth button-down shirt, and a quiet paisley tie and not get the job because the outfit whispers "Quality" but shouts "Too safe, too traditional." The challenge is to retain your own individuality and style, while looking as if you already have the job or promotion.

One of the first things you have to find out before you show up for the first day of work or for a job interview (see the section on dress in Chapter 6) is how people dress at that particular workplace. You can't assume that a white shirt and a striped tie, for example, will fit into *any* office situation.

Let's look at some specific career situations.

A Conservative Atmosphere

People who work in law firms, banks, investment firms, accounting firms, and government offices are expected to dress conservatively and traditionally because this is supposed to inspire trust. Clients expect a staff of lawyers, for example, to look authoritative and competent. In this realm, suits remain the explicit or implicit uniform. Here, too, simple, understated accessories matter. Good watches and gold or silver earrings no larger than a quarter are appropriate. Pearl stud earrings also are appropriate. Men should not wear earrings. Understated jewelry such as antique pins can add interest to a conservative suit. Makeup and hair should be low-key, understated.

Recently, I met with a young lawyer who looked wonderfully professional—great suit, fine fit, good colors. However, when I got closer, I saw that she wore no makeup whatsoever. It was jarring. Women in the corporate world cannot afford to be without, at the very least, lipstick and mascara. The greater danger, of course, lies at the other end of the spectrum—overdoing the makeup so that it looks like war paint.

Women should avoid the extremes of either flat or high heels in favor of low to midhigh heel styles. Skirts should not be shorter than the kneecaps. Busy prints of any kind work against a professional, authoritative image. And, of course, no tight skirts, dangling earrings, or bangle bracelets.

Men should not wear necklaces, bracelets, or earrings. Men's jewelry should be restricted, in fact, to a good (nondigital) watch, a wedding ring (if he is married), and/or good cuff links.

More Casual Considerations

Dress standards are somewhat different in some sales and marketing jobs, such as those with advertising and public relations firms and communications companies. These are client-intensive industries that require an appearance that has enough pizzazz and style to put people at ease yet remains authoritative and solidly representative of the company and its products. Understatement works well here. For example, a woman might choose an unmatched skirt and jacket, projecting a sense of secure style—especially if the fabric is rich and elegant. Basically, appearance for those working in these fields is not radically different than in more conservative areas. If the first thing that hits a person is your accessories or your makeup, you have gone too far.

Careers such as fashion, interior design, publishing, and cosmetics may call for a more fashion-forward and imaginative look. Turtleneck sweaters and unstructured jackets in interesting fabrics can communicate style and intelligence.

Going Informal

The health care, counseling, and teaching professions require an unintimidating look. Here, expressions of personal style are welcome because they reflect a willingness to share one's personal tastes and values. Stiff collars and the highly structured outfits appropriate for a law firm won't work for a helping professional who wants to inspire trust. On the other hand, extreme trends and high styles can be unduly intimidating.

The Code

Before you make your first appearance at a company you are visiting or joining, it is important to find out if there is a dress code.

You don't want people spending part of those crucial first few minutes wondering why you chose attire that is at odds with what is expected.

You should observe both the letter and the spirit of the code. If there is no formal code, a prime indicator is how people in senior management dress. If you follow their lead, you can't go far wrong.

To find out about a possible dress code in advance of a first visit, you can question employees, if you know any, or make a casual visit to check out the scene. Another tactic is to call the Human Resources Department and simply ask.

In some situations, a new employee might get mixed messages about what dress styles are appropriate. A recent nationwide study by Levi Strauss & Co. and the Society for Human Resource Management indicates that about 90 percent of contemporary office workers these days have the freedom to wear casual clothing, at least occasionally. If you have doubts, ask right away, even during the first important minutes, when people are making judgments about you. It shows you care enough to get things right: "I'm getting different signals from the variety of dress styles around here. Am I coming off as too conservative (or too casual)?"

Business and Social Functions

If you are invited to business functions, you will want to show up wearing what's right for each occasion. Often, your invitation will specify appropriate dress for the occasion in the lower right-hand corner. If in doubt, call your host or hostess and ask. If it is an annual affair, you might get some ideas by asking what people wore last year. You can also consult a colleague whose instincts for these things you trust by asking casually, "What are you wearing to that departmental shindig on Saturday?"

If there is a dress notation on the invitation, it will probably specify "Black tie," "Informal," or sometimes "Semiformal." *Black tie* means different things to different people all over the country. In some places, for example, a polka-dot bow tie with a dinner jacket or tuxedo is acceptable for men. Generally, it is safe for them to wear a black dinner jacket or tuxedo jacket with a black tie. (*Dinner jacket* is the correct name; *tuxedo* is the nickname.) Women have options ranging from a floor-length gown to a dressy suit in a quality fabric such as velvet, brocade, or satin. Women may or may not wear gloves, but, if they do, they never should shake hands in them. And in any affair that is at all business related, women should be cautious about an outfit that is too short or too tight or that is cut too low in the bodice.

Informal or *semiformal* calls for men to wear a dark business suit, white shirt, and a dark silk tie with a quiet pattern. Women should wear a dressy suit in an evening fabric, a short cocktail dress, or a long skirt and blouse.

For both formal and semiformal events, shoes should be highly polished or patent leather for men and fine leather or fabric for women.

Speaking of Clothing

One of the most serious and common mistakes people make when meeting others for the first time is making inappropriate comments about how the others are dressed.

Here are some guidelines:

- In the workplace, compliment people on their work rather than their clothes.

- At social functions, people do compliment one another on their outfits, simply because the nature of the occasion requires everyone to get dressed up. If someone compliments you, just say thank you. It is not necessary to return the compliment. A false compliment will have a ring of falsity to it, no matter how good an actor you think you are. You can respond by saying, "I'm glad you like it." (See the section on compliments in Chapter 13.)

- Never ask people where they got their clothes.

- Never, ever, ask someone what they paid for their clothes. If someone asks you, you can ignore the question or try to make light of it by saying, "I don't remember," and moving on to another topic.

Assembling a Wardrobe

To make a great first impression over and over again, you need a complete and well-planned wardrobe. Let's start with a couple of time-honored truisms about business attire.

- Avoid extreme fashions. No matter what the current trend setters say or do, wear what you believe is best for you and for your career, rather than what seems to be hot at the moment.

- When it comes to a decision about whether to buy two "good" items of dress or one "excellent" item, it is best to go for excellence. Quality endures and is recognized everywhere.

With these two factors in mind, the next step is to think of your wardrobe as a whole. What clothing do you need to wear to work every day? It must be appropriate to your particular corporate culture. A tweed jacket is fine on campus, but not in some boardrooms.

The overall style will be dictated not only by the particular culture of your workplace, but by what you want your attire to say about you and your company. If you want to say, "Rely on us to manage your money carefully," you don't dress in a way that says, "We're a friendly bunch of folks here."

Regional realities must be considered. Something that is just fine for Philadelphia would seem too rigid and formal in Los Angeles. Black may be best in New York, but not in Miami.

Another consideration in putting together an everyday work wardrobe is the kind of work you do. Will you be spending time on construction sites? Will you be visiting people in their homes?

Outside of the workplace, you must be ready for meeting people at social and family occasions, some of them a bit dressy and some emphatically casual.

Once you have settled on an overall style of dress, it is time to consider how you can vary your attire in ways that are interesting and that express your personality.

An Action Plan

Let's talk about building a wardrobe without breaking the bank. That's not easy for people who work in an office five days a week and live in a part of the world where seasons change, but it can be done.

Step number one is something I personally hate doing—*cleaning out the closet*. It takes a certain amount of ruthlessness.

- Dump clothes that are clearly out of style, things like really big ties, leisure suits, and Nehru jackets.

- Dump clothes that no longer fit. Since I started on a program of strength training, my upper body has changed, and certain clothes will never fit again. (Okay. If you really ARE going to lose fifteen pounds, keep that handsome suit or dress that is now too small. But don't count it as part of your basic wardrobe until such time as the fifteen pounds are history.)

- Dump those old-time favorites. They may look familiar and friendly and comfortable to you, but they will look tired to those who love them less. This is particularly true of men's shirts. A shirt is generally into its dotage after about fifty washings. So, if you have worn a shirt once a week for about a year, it is time to examine it with the cold eye of a corporate downsizer.

Once you have made these cuts, the next step is to separate the surviving items into three groups. First are the staples, including good suits, shirts, jeans, skirts, black slacks, turtlenecks. Second are things that need altering—buttons replaced, hems fixed, sleeves shortened, and so forth. Third are things that are still good, but you're tired of them: The items fit, and there's nothing wrong with them, but they need something that might make you more enthusiastic about (or at least tolerant of) them. Try adding a belt or other accessories or mixing and matching them differently.

Don't Break the Bank

In addition to your staples, every wardrobe should include a few choice blue-chip items. When making these purchases, consider the following guidelines:

- The item must be of excellent quality.
- The design should be classic and consistent with your personal style.
- You should be able to wear it often and with many different outfits.
- It should be very complimentary and very comfortable.
- Consider the "amortization" value of an item. Say you are considering buying a $300 jacket that looks great and feels great. You might want to wear it three days a week, or 121 days a year. That's about $2.50 a wearing during the first year. If the jacket lasts three years, the cost per wearing is about 80 cents.

When it comes to quality, fabric is of the utmost importance. Not long ago, only natural fibers—cotton, wool, silk, and linen—comprised "good" fabrics. Now, however, there are some terrific synthetics that blend very well with natural fibers to produce good-looking, less expensive, durable clothing. But be careful. The higher the percentage of synthetics, the fewer natural properties the fabric will have. Stay away from 100 percent polyester double knits, twills, or gabardines; obviously acrylic knits; simulated leather; and phony silks. The bottom line with fabrics is feel. It is a good idea, when you have doubts about the quality of a fabric, to do a touch comparison with other fabrics: Crush the fabric in your hand; if it springs back unharmed, chances are it will serve you well.

Here are some things to look for when shopping for quality:

- The better a garment is made on the inside, the better it will wear. Check the seams and the lining.
- Buttons should be securely sewn and should meet buttonholes squarely. Colors should match perfectly. In a heavy garment, there should be a stem between the button and the fabric.
- Zippers should be neatly concealed and the same color as the fabric, and they should work flawlessly.
- Jackets should fit squarely. Back vents and collars should lie flat and not pucker.
- Patterns should match at the seams, collars, and pockets.
- Double-breasted jackets should have inside buttons and buttonholes to hold the line of the garment.

Although it is important to look for sales and to comparison shop, it is also important to build a relationship with a store where you feel comfortable and with a professional in that store. This person will not only help you put together a look that is right for you but can alert you to upcoming sales and provide other advice and information. (It's also a good idea to develop a relationship with a good dry cleaner, tailor, and cobbler.)

SUITable

For Men

Quality fabric, fit, proportion, and color are the important considerations in choosing a suit. Fads and flourishes are inappropriate in most business venues.

Double-breasted suits are generally considered a bit too fashion-forward for traditional corporate modes. It's best to acquire a wardrobe of traditional two-button suits before venturing into the double-breasted arena. Men who are even the slightest bit portly shouldn't even consider double-breasted suits. It simply adds a layer of fabric around the middle, where they can least afford it.

Consider scale and proportion. Shorter men look better with two-button spacing. Taller men can wear four-button spacing with somewhat broader lapels. The waist button of a jacket should be just below the narrowest part of the torso. Men with athletic builds—wide shoulders, narrow waist and hips—look far better in double-breasted suits. However, it's a good idea to find out if any other men in the company wear double-breasted before making a purchase.

Collars can help balance facial features, softening rigid lines and giving strength to soft ones. For example, straight-point collars balance a round, heavy face, and spread collars offset a long, narrow face.

Pleated trousers these days generally are considered not only dressier but more comfortable. The classic pleat design has a deep pleat near the fly and a shallower one nearer the pocket. Pants should rest with a slight break on the shoe. Cuffs, of perhaps an inch, give the pant legs just enough weight to help define the pleat and keep contact with the shoe.

For men, one of the most important details is the necktie. If people remember only one thing about what you are wearing, it could very easily be that tie. A striped tie is always classic, but fashion is moving more toward foulards with tiny, spaced geometric forms, prints, and patterns. Paisley prints are upscale and rich looking. The most fashion-forward are the boldly colored, geometric ties. The most useful colors are dark blue, olive, teal blue, purple, taupe and every shade of red.

If you wear braces (sometimes misnamed "suspenders"), don't wear a belt. Most often, braces are made of silk with leather fittings. The color and pattern should coordinate with the shirt and tie.

For Women

No longer must women wear a feminized version of men's business attire to climb the corporate ladder. These days, women in business have the option of dressing in more colorful, varied, and feminine ways.

Man-tailored suits are being replaced with blazers and collarless jackets and pantsuits. Top quality pantsuits in sober, businesslike colors are accepted in most business climates these days. When they fit correctly, they are more modest and comfortable than skirts and look better than skirts with low-heeled shoes. Women who are wider in the hips should make sure the jacket is long enough to completely cover the hips, thus producing a slimmer line. Very slim-hipped women can get away with a short jacket.

Suits can project approachability or rigidity simply by virtue of their fabric and color. Stiff fabrics such as gabardine convey inflexibility when they are in dark colors such as black or navy. Loosely constructed suits make others feel more at ease, and bright colors suggest lively thinking. For example, I rarely wear rigidly constructed suits with both parts matching in color simply because of the nature of what I teach. The subject of etiquette is intimidating enough by itself, and I want to help bridge that bias with what I'm wearing.

To decide on the appropriateness of skirt length, take a long, objective look in a three-way mirror, then sit down in front of the same mirror. If you have even the slightest doubt, the skirt is too short. Generally, the most flattering place to end a hemline is at the slimmest part of the leg. Most often, that's where the calf meets the knee in a graceful curve. Straight skirts usually look best when they are just covering the knee. Full skirts and pleated skirts look best when they are much longer, perhaps even nearly ankle-length.

And don't think you can just whack off six inches from a suit skirt because the fashion that year is short skirts. See a good tailor first. If shortening destroys the proportions of a skirt, it is better to recycle it at a thrift shop or jazz it up with new accessories. Remember that most classic lengths do not go out of style.

Long, slim skirts may seem sophisticated yet aloof. Full, long skirts make a woman look expansive and approachable. Swinging short pleated skirts make a person look more fluid and easygoing. Long jackets over short skirts add an air of professionalism and sophistication.

Women's collars can send a variety of messages. For example, asymmetrical and very pointed collars suggest a creative person. Unbuttoned collars speak of flexible open-mindedness. Large, dramatic collars suggest authority, power, and dynamism. Tiny Peter Pan collars do not convey authority. You should avoid crumpled and floppy collars completely; they suggest that you are lacking in competence. If your collars are too rigid, pointed, and starched, they can suggest that you are the same way.

Accessories

For Men

A man's accessories can do a lot for his image. He should go for an alligator or crocodile belt. Starched linen pocket handkerchiefs add authority. Small gold or sterling silver cuff links add quiet presence. An elegant dress watch is a worthwhile investment. Stay away from bulky sports watches, digital watches, and those with cheap metal bands, jewels, or Mickey Mouse-type icons. Wear only wedding or signet rings. Class rings are passé, and diamond rings are verboten. (Tiffany won't even make a man's diamond ring.) Men in the business arena should never wear earrings, pinkie rings, bracelets, or necklaces.

For Women

Women's accessories usually mean scarves, belts, and jewelry. Scarves, however, operate against women when they must be adjusted constantly. If you can't tie a scarf or drape it in ways that require no readjustment, then avoid them.

Belts should be of fine leather. Alligator or crocodile belts are always elegant, if not politically correct. Suede also adds rich texture. Wear very wide belts only if you are a very thin, long-waisted woman. Otherwise, go for inch-wide belts with handsome buckles.

Belts do not have to match shoes, although they should be in the same color family. The quietest ones are the most elegant. Leave the advertising logos to the adolescents.

Generally, earrings about the size of a quarter work best in business. They are large enough to be important and authoritative, yet small enough not to be distracting. Of course, if you are petite, choose something smaller. Drop earrings do not look professional. A good pair of real gold earrings is a worthy investment. The same goes for real pearls. But excellent costume jewelry is available today, and losing an earring is less painful when it's not 18-carat gold.

A basic rule is that jewelry should not be obtrusive or vulgarly ostentatious. Save your emeralds for the grand ball.

Avoid wearing rings on your right hand. You will feel less dread about a crunching handshake, and you won't have to worry about a ring digging into the other person's fingers.

Fur may be appropriate to wear to the office if your home office is in Reykjavík (Iceland). For the most part, however, the message that fur sends in a business setting is "pretentious," not "successful."

For Both Men and Women

Eyeglasses can make a person look authoritative, intense, and serious. When I was younger, I often wore glasses when lecturing, even though I didn't need them, on the theory that people would take me more seriously. Tortoiseshell glasses can be more serviceable than silver or gold frames because they won't clash with any jewelry. I recently received an e-mail question about whether a man could wear silver frames with a gold watch to a job interview. The answer is, certainly—unless it made him feel uncomfortable, in which case he probably wouldn't perform well.

Leather gloves with dull finishes bespeak quality. Also, it's a good idea to wear thin gloves so that you don't ruin coats by stuffing heavy gloves into the pockets.

Sure you love your faithful old briefcase, but when it gets to be shabby looking, retire it to the same closet as the teddy bears and school sweater, and buy yourself a new one. Fine leather briefcases are a wise investment. Actually, having two briefcases is the ideal—a slim one for meetings and a larger, possibly soft-sided one for travels back and forth from the office. In the slim one, carry only those documents necessary for the meeting, projecting focus, authority, and attention to detail.

Shoes

Shoes are such an important (and necessary) accessory that they deserve special consideration. You don't often see your shoes, but others do. And shoes that are not properly cared for send a negative message.

With shoes (as with neckties), you should buy the best you can afford. Look for high-quality leather.

Most women can create a perfectly thorough shoe wardrobe with a pair each of black, tan, and navy blue.

Pumps with low heels are the most elegant and serviceable, and they are often the most flattering.

Women should never, ever wear running shoes anywhere near the business arena. Fortunately, many shoe manufacturers are producing good-looking leather pumps that are well cushioned and comfortable even for walking long distances or for being on one's feet for long periods of time.

Here are some helpful shoe facts particularly for men:

- The dressier the shoe, the thinner the sole and heel.
- Uppers should be of shiny and supple leather, and there should be four pairs of eyelets for the laces.
- Lace-up shoes are called oxfords.
- Black wingtips are rather formal and are exactly appropriate for pinstripe suits and any dress navy or gray suit.
- Suede shoes can be very costly. They are popular in London, but their elegance is underappreciated in the United States.
- Classic loafers are entirely appropriate in business and work well with everything but the most formal blue business suit. They used to be called penny loafers but, thankfully, the pennies are long gone. Tasseled loafers have tassels instead of the penny band. They look quite formal in black, but they are not suitable for formal wear. Kilt loafers are similar to tassel loafers except that they have a fringe of leather instead of the tassel.

⊞

A buyer for a department store chain once shared with me some advice she received while training for her job.

"When you meet someone, take a look at her handbag and shoes, and you'll know what you are dealing with."

Start out with your shoes looking right, and keep some fabric softening sheets and/or a shoe brush in your desk for minor rebuffing.

⊞

You might say that the impact of clothing is felt even before you actually meet someone new. People are aware of what you are wearing even as you approach them.

There is no such thing as neutral clothing, and there is no business "uniform" that is appropriate for all places and situations. So what you wear requires a great deal of careful thought and not a little common sense.

What you wear makes a statement about you. Think about what you want that statement to be, and dress accordingly.

5

Good Grooming

I entered the Center City store intent on buying a handbag. The clerk, an attractive young woman, greeted me with a smile and a "May I help you?"

My first impression was entirely favorable, and I was ready to do business. Then, as I began speaking, the clerk started cleaning the fingernails of her right hand with the fingernails of her left hand and flicking the results of the effort in the direction of the floor.

I temporarily lost interest in handbags and left the store.

If you ask a group of people to list the things that, for them, create an instant negative reaction on meeting someone, they might begin the list with things like:

- Hair that is dirty or unruly.
- Too much makeup.
- Dirty fingernails.

The lists might be long, but odds are that the first item on every one of them will involve grooming. It's more important than dress when it comes to making that favorable first impression. The effect of an elegant, perfectly fitted outfit can be utterly negated by poor grooming.

Grooming is more important than what you say. In fact, the person who is registering the fact that your nails are chipped or dirty probably won't be paying that much attention to what you are saying.

So, before you think about what you will wear or what you will say, make sure you have dealt thoroughly with every detail of good grooming.

It almost goes without saying that scrupulous cleanliness is absolutely vital. For men, stubble is unacceptable except under the most extraordinary circumstances. It's a good idea to keep shaving gear in your desk or briefcase for emergencies. Use of deodorants is a must, but avoid deodorants with a strong smell, and stay away from heavy colognes.

Make Up for It

Women shouldn't make the mistake of thinking that going without makeup entirely will make them look real or natural. It will not. It will make them look washed-out and unfinished. Makeup is a necessary and very important part of the grooming package that helps women make that favorable first impression.

The two basic makeup rules are:

1. Less is more.
2. Simpler is better.

Every business woman needs some makeup. This does not mean spending long hours in front of the mirror applying paint. Your routine should take no more than five or ten minutes.

It is a wise investment to have a makeup lesson from a professional. Usually, they sell their own products, which can get to be expensive. However, I've found that buying them actually saves me money in the long run because I'm never captured at a department store cosmetic counter buying sixty-five items I didn't know I needed until I saw them there.

Having a professional instruct you on how to apply everything provides a gold mine of information that often comes free when you purchase the makeup. Most reputable beauty salons have a professional aesthetician on staff who does skin care and makeup. Most of the large cosmetic companies often do makeovers at stores at no charge.

Your basic career makeup should include a bit of foundation to even out face color, some eye shadow, a bit of eyeliner for definition, lip liner and lipstick, powder on the shiny parts of the face—in the center of the forehead, nose, and chin—a dusting of blush, and some mascara.

It's a good idea to start with your eyes. Beauty experts suggest designing your eyebrows, eyes, and lip line to match the shape of your eyes. For example, if your eyes are round, give a round shape to your brows and lips. The same principle goes for almond-shaped eyes. This way, the various parts of your face look as if they belong together, and the symmetry accentuates the features with which you were born.

And the eyes have it when it comes to making decisions about lipstick, eye makeup, and blush. If you have brown eyes, look for colors with brown, orange, or yellow undertones and reds ranging from medium to dark. Avoid mauve or blue undertones. However, mauve and blue or mauve and rose undertones go well with blue eyes, as do light pink to fuchsia, pink, and reds. Rose and burgundy or brown undertones go well with hazel and green eyes, which also favor reds with rose, burgundy, or brown undertones. Women of color will look good with both blue and orange undertones, deep reds with blue, wine or brown undertones. Asian eyes are complemented by rose and wine undertones and reds with blue or wine undertones.

Do some testing. Your best color will seem to give your face a healthy glow. It will smooth out your skin and mitigate or eliminate shadows and lines.

Hair: Crown or Frown

The first and overriding rule is that hair must always be clean and well groomed.

There has always been ambivalence about long hair versus short hair for women. I think that as long as a woman's hair is clean, out of her face, and off her shoulders, she can look professional. A colleague of mine has a long, flowing mane of chestnut hair. For business, she wears it pulled tightly back in a long braid, and it looks wonderful. Granted, this is not a style that all of us can successfully adopt.

Most women look best in a combination of long and short hair—a little longer here, a little shorter there. That's what a good cut and good styling can do. When you make an appointment with a stylist, the consultation often comes with it at no charge.

A good general styling rule is that it's the size of the face and not so much the shape of the face that matters. For example, a tiny face will look overwhelmed and overshadowed by a lot of hair, and someone with a very large head and face needs ample hair for balance and would look out of proportion with a buzzed cut.

And only in Hollywood can you get away with the black roots-light hair look. If roots are a problem, don't ignore them. There are a number of touchup products on the market.

On the Face of It

For men, putting their best face forward can involve some tough decisions about facial hair.

On the one hand, facial hair can make a young man look a little older and can disguise a receding chin or lips that are too thin. On the other hand, some senior executives find facial hair offensive or, at least, ostentatious. If possible, check out the appearance of men in a particular professional or business situation before you make a decision about facial hair.

If you have grown a beard to cover scarring or if there are other good reasons for facial hair, keep it. If you are undecided, the safer alternative is to get rid of it.

If you DO decide to sport facial hair, don't be theatrical about it. I tend to think that handlebar mustaches look silly, and goatees look satanic, but they are enjoying a trendy comeback these days, particularly in the more creative career fields. Whichever style you chose, facial hair must always look well tended.

Your Nails

All of us should be aware that our hands are constantly on display. Bad-looking nails will almost certainly be noticed within seconds of your meeting with a new person.

Invest in at least one good manicure as a learning experience. After that, you probably can handle the job yourself. This goes for men as well as women. Some men have to get over the idea that a manicure is somehow unmasculine.

One trick a manicurist taught me was to dip my fingers into a lemon or grapefruit to remove stains. It works, feels good, is cheap, and smells great afterward.

Good nails indicate good health. They must be cleaned and shaped with cuticles pushed back and trimmed. Avoid the "Morticia" look, with long, red or black talons. Clear polish is a safe bet for business use, and it is also the easiest to maintain because it doesn't chip easily and when it does, the chips don't show.

Your Skin

Don't ignore basic skin care. Both men and women should regularly cleanse their skin and exfoliate to remove dead skin. I recommend that people cleanse, rinse, and moisturize twice a day and exfoliate weekly. There are plenty of good, moderately priced products at the drugstore. Drinking lots of water is important in helping to avoid a dehydrated look.

Looking Great

Nothing enhances your overall appearance like being fit. A good regimen of exercise will improve not only your posture but your personality. I believe that fit people look more focused and more confident.

A recent national survey showed that a majority of working women interviewed believe that becoming physically fit and participating in sports will help their careers.

Exercise not only increases strength and endurance, but I find it also helps to defuse anger and frustration, and it gets the creative juices flowing. I run, row crew, and pump iron on a regular basis, and it pays wonderful dividends.

⁘

It is not enough to be freshly showered and neatly combed. Good grooming also means attention to detail. No amount of time and effort in this department is wasted.

Not only can grooming make or break any effort to make a good first impression, it will leave a lasting impression. People will remember bad makeup or dirty fingernails long after they have forgotten whether your necktie complemented your suit color.

6

Job Interview

Meg Sanders is trying not to fiddle with her scarf, pick at imaginary lint on her jacket, squirm, or scratch. And she worries that her hand will be moist when it comes time to shake.

Because this is IT, the interview for the job she wants very much, a job that can open the door to a future she wants very much.

She sits on a hard plastic chair, being ignored by the receptionist, and, as an antisquirm/antiscratch tactic, she mentally goes over what she has done to get ready for this encounter.

She reminds herself of the two key factors working for her:

- The company is looking for potential employees, or it would not be interviewing people.
- The person conducting the interview is hoping that she, Meg Sanders, will be someone the company wants to hire.

Is She Ready?

Meg has, of course, been especially careful about dress and grooming, which count for so much during those first few minutes when that crucial first impression is formed.

She has learned everything she can about the company, beginning with a trip to the library and a look at publications such as Moody's manuals, Fitch Corporation manuals, McRae's *Bluebook* and Standard & Poor's *Register*.

She is confident about the pronunciation of the company name and the name of the interviewer. She knows what the company does, how large it is, whether it's national or international, how long it has been around, and its general reputation.

She has talked to company employees and others to learn as much as possible about the company's corporate culture, particularly how people in management dress and whether the overall style is casual or formal.

She has made an exploratory visit, learning how long it takes to get to the company headquarters and exactly how to reach the office where the interview will take place. This visit also can help her to form an idea about how people dress. This is an area where guesswork can be a fatal mistake. Khakis and loafers may be appropriate in one place, whereas double-breasted suits and wing tips are best for another. (If you need to, it is perfectly fine to call the human resources office and ask about this. When in doubt, dress more formally rather than more casually.)

The job interview, of course, is a situation in which impeccable grooming is an absolute necessity. Very careful attention must be paid to things like hair and nails, and clothing must be fresh, pressed, and appropriate. (See Chapters 4 and 5, which concern dress and grooming.)

Self-Research

Meg's research also has included a thorough look at herself, and she is prepared to talk about her education, honors, and awards; volunteer work; interests and hobbies; the abilities she can bring to his job; and the reason she wants to work for the company.

She has even gone so far as to do some role-playing about the interview with a friend, tape-recording the session and listening to it later.

The Encounter

So, Meg figures she is about as ready as she can be when, finally, one of two things happens:

1. The receptionist says to Meg, "Ms. Gilbert will see you now."
2. Ms. Gilbert comes out of her office to fetch Meg.

In the latter case, Meg stands up and smiles, makes eye contact, and is prepared to shake hands, which means her briefcase or other materials are in her left hand or on a chair or table. She will more or less follow Gilbert to her office, and if Gilbert stands aside to let Meg enter first, she will do so without hesitation.

If Gilbert does not come out to greet her, Meg enters the office purposefully and with good posture. She does not take a seat until she is asked to do so. She sits straight, all the way back in the chair with both feet on the floor, briefcase on the floor beside the chair, and files, if any, on her lap.

Shifting Gears

At this moment, Meg Sanders stops thinking about herself and starts thinking about the interviewer. Gilbert may be asking about things like job experience and educational background, but what she really wants is to get a feeling for Meg's personality, her trainability, and her potential for success.

Answering Questions

Meg is resolved to be completely truthful about everything. Deceptions have a way of coming back at you, and a trained interviewer will immediately spot any effort to fudge over or minimize any negative facts. Complete candor, on the other hand, conveys the impression that this is someone who can be trusted.

"Why did you leave your last job?" Ms. Gilbert asks.

Meg replies, "Frankly, it was because of a basic disagreement with the owner. I believed our operation could be greatly streamlined by using some new techniques. The boss said it was his way or the highway, so I decided to look elsewhere."

She says this without any accusation or emotion in her voice.

When the complicated or difficult questions come along, Meg does not rush in with an answer, even though she may have one prepared. She is more comfortable and makes a better impression if she takes a moment to think before she answers. When she answers, she looks right at Gilbert and not at her hands or the ceiling. When the interviewer pauses, Meg resists the temptation to fill in the silence with babble.

Screening Interviews

Meg's interview is with the person who will be making the decision about whether to hire her. Often, however, the first interview with a company representative will be a screening interview. It is important to remember that the purpose of a screening interview is to screen OUT applicants.

In a screening interview, the interviewer has in mind such basic questions as:

- Does this person dress well enough and speak well enough to join the company?
- Does the person have the minimal educational background?
- Is the person willing to relocate if necessary?

Most screening interviews are done in person, but sometimes a screening interview will be done over the telephone or even by teleconferencing. If so, make sure you have all your materials close at hand. If, for any reason, an interview call catches you unprepared or unable to speak at any length, get the name and number of the interviewer and call back as promptly as possible.

If you are contacted for a teleconferencing interview, you will need to go to a local Kinko's store or other facility to be interviewed on camera.

Here are some tips for a video interview:

- Don't let the camera rattle you. Remember that for the recruiter, this is still just a routine screening interview. Don't think of it as an audition. You don't have to perform for the camera.
- If possible, ask for a preliminary telephone conversation to establish some rapport.
- Arrive early and familiarize yourself with the equipment. In some situations, the candidates can adjust volume, brightness, and other camera functions with a remote. Once the interview begins, forget the remote.
- Sit up straight, take your time, and speak normally.
- Treat the camera as if it were the recruiter. Look at it when speaking.
- Because of transmission lags, the voice may be out of sync with the picture. Don't let it throw you.

The Final Interview

Experienced Interviewer

In the case of larger companies, the person conducting the final interview very likely will have training in interview techniques and/or considerable experience in interviewing potential new employees. This means the interview is likely to follow a fairly predictable course, starting with a few pleasantries: "Did you get caught in the rain?" or "Is this your first visit to Cleveland?"

Next will be questions about and references to the material in the resume, education and previous jobs, for example.

Then comes what might be called the "essay questions":

"Why are you interested in joining this company (or following this career path) in particular?"

"What are your long-range (or short-range) goals?"

"Tell me about yourself."

This is no place for half-hearted responses and negative or vague language.

Here are some **wrong** answers:

- "I heard the company has pretty good benefits."
- "I was never really good at math and science, so I've concentrated on the creative side."
- "I guess my short-range goal is to get this job and see how it works out."

And some **right** answers:

- "I'm COMMITTED to learning and to being successful."
- "I ENJOY research."

Note that these answers use positive, active language.

67

Inexperienced Interviewer

These same precepts also apply during interviews with an untrained and inexperienced person, such as the owner of a small firm.

This person may be vague and prone to ask unfocused or seemingly irrelevant questions. He is casting a broad net for information or perhaps just keeping the conversation going while he is waiting for his intuition to kick in and tell him what to decide about the person with whom he is talking. He is probably looking for a "certain something" that may not be fully articulated in his own mind.

Whether he knows it or not, some of the things he is looking for are energy, honesty, and a positive attitude. These are things that are reflected in a person's positive speech, posture, and body language.

Thank You Note

Finally, follow up interviews immediately with a handwritten thank you note to the interviewer. In addition to thanking the interviewer for his or her time, it is helpful to refer to something that occurred during the meeting, if possible. Only type if your handwriting is illegible.

Dear Ms. Gilbert:

Thank you for seeing me on Thursday to discuss the opening in the Marketing Department at Micro-Word. It was a pleasure to meet you, and I enjoyed learning more about the company and its plans for the future.

I hope to hear from you soon.

Sincerely,
Meg Sanders
Meg Sanders

It is best to think of the job interview as an opportunity rather than as a test. It is helpful to keep in mind that the reason for the interview is that the company or the person wants to hire someone and is probably hoping that you are the one.

The more preparation you have, the better. Even if it turns out that some of the effort that went into the preparation was unnecessary, the fact that you have done it will help you to be more relaxed and confident during the interview. When in doubt:

- Tell the complete truth.
- Dress more formally than more casually.
- Don't be shy about mentioning your achievements and interests, but don't repeat. The interviewer heard you the first time.

7

The Business Meeting

The new Human Resources Department head, Pam Thompson, is paying particular attention to Allen Devlin and Wes Worthington as they arrive for this morning's meeting. Thompson is preparing to appoint a new deputy department head, somebody who will take over the day-to-day operation of her department. Based on their records, Devlin and Worthington are the most likely candidates.

She looks them over as they enter the room. Both are well dressed, in their midthirties, and apparently hard-working and knowledgeable. The two men enter the room with an equal chance at the job. They leave it ninety minutes later with Devlin running a distant second.

Devlin made a negative impression during the first few minutes and did little during the rest of the meeting to reverse that impression. He arrived looking distracted; he failed to greet or speak to anyone; and he seated himself in the chair next to Thompson, the one she had been saving for her administrative assistant. During the course of the meeting, he twice interrupted Worthington's interesting and well-structured presentation with questions that could have waited until the end. He wasted a lot of time shuffling papers when it came time for him to report on the Albright contract.

But the biggest factor was the overall impression he made during the meeting: He slouched. He spread his briefcase and papers all over the table. He bent and straightened no fewer than five paper clips, snapped a rubber band, and at one point removed his jacket and draped it over the back of his chair.

This kind of behavior is typical of those who think of meetings as an interruption of their work, a sort of purgatory of boredom where nothing of any substance gets done. But presenting yourself at meetings creates fine opportunities for making a solid, favorable impression. It is at these sessions that people learn about one another and make judgments about one another.

Showing Up Ready to Go

Always arrive on time or even a little early for a meeting. Arriving late is insulting to those who took the trouble to arrive on time. Others in the room, consciously or otherwise, will feel a modicum of resentment toward you.

Also, dashing in at the last minute does not convey the impression that you are a dynamic, busy person, only that you are disorganized.

If you cannot avoid being late, apologize as soon as it is convenient and give the reason, succinctly: "I'm sorry I'm late. Mr. Chamberlain said he had to speak to me right away, and you know that when he says right away, he means it."

Enter the room decisively and, while still standing, shake hands with your colleagues. Smile, and call people by their names. Introduce yourself to those you don't know. If you are seated and a new introduction is made, stand up.

And it is usually a good idea to use honorifics when addressing others at meetings, even if you are on a first-name basis with the person at other times. However, this will depend ultimately on the corporate style of your organization. Once again, when in doubt, formal is better than informal.

Unless you are certain about seating arrangements, ask where you should sit. If it's "sit anywhere," don't sit at either end of the table. If you know where the chairman or senior officer present will be sitting, don't sit right next to him because these places may be reserved for chief aides or a secretary.

Arrive ready to work, bringing agenda, papers, notebook, and pens. Have what you think you will need at hand so that you don't keep people waiting while you fish around for things that should be in front of you.

Put briefcases and purses on the floor and not on spare chairs or, worse, on the conference table.

Don't play. Leave paper clips unbent, rubber bands unstretched and unsnapped. Don't doodle on your notepad.

Don't ask for coffee or other refreshments unless they are being offered. If there is food or drinks at the meeting, get rid of your cup and/or plate as soon as you conveniently can. Aside from a possible glass of water, your place at the conference table should be clear.

Watching Your Body Language

One of Devlin's big mistakes was letting his body language send out all the wrong messages. You want to look relaxed but attentive, and yes, it is possible to sit straight without slouching and still be relaxed. Keep your feet on the floor for the most part. If you cross your legs, do so at the ankles. Avoid crossing your arms in front of you. It communicates resistance, even hostility. Your body language should communicate an open mind, approachability.

Keep your jacket and tie on unless the person in charge of the meeting sheds his and strongly suggests that others do the same.

You might want to pick up a copy of *Robert's Rules of Order* and familiarize yourself with this universally recognized guide to meeting procedure. Of course, it is used only at the most formal meetings, but someday you may be at a meeting and someone will say, "How should we proceed with this?" You could then say, "Well, *Robert's Rules of Order* suggests . . ." Even if it never happens, you know you will be ready in case it does.

Speaking Up for Yourself

"Allen, will you tell us the latest on the Albright situation?"

"Huh? Oh, yeah. Let me see here. Okay. I talked with Mr. Albright . . . when was it? Wednesday. No, Thursday. Anyway, he says . . ."

Even the most minor players are likely to be called upon to say something at a meeting. Be ready. Try to predict in advance what the subject will be, decide what you will say, and mentally practice your remarks. You won't look surprised and confused when called on, and you will be less likely to ramble and to repeat yourself.

When it comes time for you to say something, don't stand up unless people routinely stand while speaking at the meeting. Take a second or two to frame your first sentence in your mind. Get right to the point and be as brief as possible: "Mr. Albright is prepared to agree to the terms suggested by the legal department, but he wants some assurance that the work will be done promptly. I convinced him that we can foresee no delays, and the project should go forward without a hitch."

Avoid repetition but, if it is a point you feel must be emphasized through repetition, say something like: "I'm repeating this point because I think it is so important."

Use positive language, and never begin with an apology for what you will say. Avoid such phrases as: "This might not work, but . . ."

State your position clearly and firmly, but stop pressing it or defending it when the chairman or the boss says, "Okay, here's what we're going to do . . ." or "Let's move on to another topic."

Watch your language. Use the pronoun "we" when discussing the work or the position of your company or your department. You will come across as a team player when things are going well, and it will help to take the focus off you when things are not going so well. Make suggestions and bring up "points to consider" rather than taking inflexible positions. Avoid confrontational language: "I disagree because . . ." is better than "You're wrong about that."

Don't interrupt while others are speaking, no matter how much you disagree with what is being said.

The Chair

The importance of the first impression you make at a meeting is multiplied many times when you are chairing the meeting because so much of the attention will be focused on you so much of the time.

Once again, preparation is crucial. Provide as much advance notice as you can, and to the degree that it is possible, pick a time that is convenient for everyone. Avoid Friday afternoon and Monday morning. Consider the jobs and the schedules of the participants when scheduling the meeting. If the meeting is lengthy, provide breaks so that people can make telephone calls and attend to personal needs.

Think about seating. Pick the head or the middle of the table for yourself. You may want to reserve the chairs on either side of you for your most important guests or for those with whom you will be working most closely at the meeting.

If a specific seating arrangement is desired, you can use name cards. These should be two-sided with the names on both sides. Do not use Mr., Ms., or Mrs., but use Dr. where appropriate. Each place at the table should have a supply of notepaper, pencils, and whatever else might be needed. Find out in advance if there will be a need for a lectern, a microphone, a blackboard or a whiteboard, audiovisual aids, or a copier.

If it is to be a lengthy meeting, you may want to provide simple snacks or lunch. Avoid anything greasy, such as chips, or anything difficult to eat. Make low-fat and vegetarian alternatives available, and provide decaffeinated tea and coffee as well as regular and pitchers or bottles of water.

Style and Structure

If you are chairing the meeting, you want to do everything possible to establish an atmosphere in which frank, open, and creative discussion will flourish. If you encourage creative debate, it's your job to intervene before a situation gets heated and out of hand: "Evan and Carol both have good points, and they argue them well. Now, let's try to move toward some kind of consensus."

Other tactics include simply calling on someone else for an opinion or putting the hot subject aside until the combatants have cooled down.

Be sure to distribute the agenda and other paperwork pertaining to the meeting well in advance. The agenda should begin with the time and the place of the meeting and the names of the chairperson and the others who are expected to attend. The most important issues should be handled first in case the meeting runs out of time. If the meeting is to occur at mealtime, include a phrase such as "Sandwiches and beverages will be provided" on the agenda.

A useful way to control the length of the meeting and to keep things moving is to write times with the topics on the agenda. For example:

- Review quarterly goals and action plan—30 minutes
- Discuss publicity campaign for new product—20 minutes
- Establish priorities and goals for Atco design project—20 minutes
- Open discussion—15 minutes

- Conclusion: summary and action-plan assignments—
20 minutes

Outside Directorships

If you are asked to serve on the board of directors of a charitable or community organization, you may find that the meetings take on an entirely different character than those within your company.

Such appointments can be important career opportunities, but these meetings can be fraught with dangers and complexities. It very well may be that your boss or whomever asked you to take on the appointment has friends or close business associations on the same board. In any case, it is likely that your performance on the board and at its meetings will get back to your home company.

It's up to you to find out, through careful observation, about the procedures and rules for acceptable behavior at these outside meetings.

Suppose you have been asked to serve on the board of a charitable or cultural organization. You may find yourself on a board composed of a rather diverse set of people toting some diverse attitudinal baggage. Some may be wealthy dilettantes dabbling in the arts or community affairs. Some may be scholars or artists. Some may be representatives of the communities that the charity represents. There may even be a retired business tycoon who "knows how to get things done." Some will have unspoken agendas that have little or nothing to do with the work of the organization.

The strategy for making the correct first impression in these situations requires that you go slowly at first. Start out by being cordial but somewhat reserved, at least until you get a handle on how relationships work on the board. Again, more formal is better than less formal. Make it clear from the beginning that you belong to no clique and won't take sides.

When appropriate, offer to help the head of the organization with contacts and access to special information. If you can provide something that is lacking, such as computer expertise, volunteer to do so. Keep good notes. If you make promises, be sure to follow up with action as promptly as possible.

Don't be a half-hearted or faint-hearted volunteer. Be a cheerleader back at the office for the group or the charity. Speak proudly about its good works. If you can do so without annoying people, muster up some support from your company. Buy at least two tickets to your charity's benefits, and try to get your company to buy a table as a corporate sponsor. Remember to repay the volunteers who organize these benefits in the currency of thanks and praise.

Meeting etiquette is like stage lighting. You only notice it when it's bad. The simple act of attending a meeting is an opportunity to give a positive first impression to a number of people at once. Just the act of being quiet and listening attentively to others makes a favorable impression.

8

Office Tactics

The techniques and the strategies for making a good first impression come into play on an everyday basis around the office.

Not only are you meeting new people who come into the workplace, but the roles of your co-workers are constantly changing, and when that happens, your relationship with them not only changes but, in effect, starts over. For example, you have met Lisa Elkton, regional supervisor, in the past. But the first time you meet Lisa Elkton, vice president, it's a whole new ball game. In effect, you are seeing each other with new eyes.

And there are times, such as when you are being considered for a promotion or as a candidate for a certain position or project, when people who were previously unaware of or indifferent to your behavior, appearance, and style will begin observing you and forming a first impression.

Beyond all of that, when you spend several hours daily in the same place with the same people, little annoyances can become infuriating. Boorish behavior can become insufferable. That's why it is a good idea to bring to your daily activities in the workplace some of the tactics and the techniques that you would use to make a favorable first impression during the first few minutes of meeting someone new. Successful people know that, in the workplace, you must be able to make that good first impression over and over again.

Relations with your staff, colleagues, and bosses will be somewhat different, of course, but all three will have the same two cornerstones—respect and consideration.

Being an Unbossy Boss

A cordial and considerate attitude toward your support staff must be evident from the first time you meet them. Not only will they be working closely with you every day, but they are key factors in how effectively you function.

When setting the tone for your relationship, remember that when in doubt, more formal is better than less formal. Always greet them pleasantly, making a good first impression on a daily basis. Always acknowledge their presence.

Let's say you are speaking with your assistant or your secretary, and someone else joins you. Here is an important first-impressions situation. When you introduce them, make the introduction according to the way those two will be addressing each other in the future. If you are introducing your secretary to a client and you wish the secretary to address the client as Mr. Toomey in the future, that's how you introduce him: "Mr. Toomey, this is my secretary, Ms. Greer."

In this situation, you use the secretary's surname as well as Toomey's, even if you use the secretary's first name at other times.

At your first meeting with those who will work for you, make it clear how you wish to be addressed: "Hello, Ms. Greer. I'm John Hanley."

Never give yourself an honorific.

If Ms. Greer calls you by your first name and you do not wish her to, it will be necessary to say, "Ms. Greer, I think it will work better if we address each other by our surnames."

And whatever form of address you use, *never, ever* refer to anyone as "honey," "handsome," "girl," "boy," or any other such term. Learn and use the person's name.

Be careful about asking support staff to perform personal errands. For one thing, they may resent non-work-related orders. If they take their complaint to a senior executive, it will reflect unfavorably on your professionalism. It could also lead to them assuming a level of familiarity that you will find inappropriate or uncomfortable.

Be wary of exceeding a subordinate's reasonable workload. If you are sharing a secretary, consult with your associate so that you both can be sure that you are not piling on more work than the secretary can handle.

Peer Points

Some people seem to think it's a good idea to immediately begin treating a new co-worker as if they had grown up together.

When dealing with colleagues or peers, let the relationship evolve at its own pace. Do not assume that a certain level of familiarity exists between the two of you because you both do the same work or even share the same facilities and resources.

Say, for example, you are introduced to a new staffer, Barbara Williams. You put out your hand, smile, make eye contact and say, "It's nice to meet you."

Right here is where you need to make a judgment call. If you are operating in a decidedly conservative business culture, you will say "It's nice to meet you, Ms. Williams," with the expectation that her reply would include, "Please call me Barbara." In most business situations, however, you will address a peer using the first name.

Next, you ask if there is anything you can do to help her get settled and let her know where you can be found if she has any questions or needs any help.

It is a good rule of thumb to remember that the person who is your equal today could be your boss tomorrow.

Superior Treatment

As for your bosses, don't be fooled by an appearance of casual friendliness or cheerful, offhand greetings. Relationships in the American business world are based on rank, and rank should always be observed and acknowledged. Just because the boss has invited you to use his or her first name or has invited you along for lunch or a golf outing, don't assume that you are now buddies. You can go along with the style set by the boss to some degree, but don't lose sight of the realities. Whether you call the boss "Ms. Gallagher" or "Margaret," she's still the boss.

Hosting Visitors

When someone comes into your office, even for a casual visit, you are the host and should make the visitor welcome. Once again, the first few minutes are crucial.

If it is someone who routinely stops by, it may not be necessary for you to get up and greet the person formally. But you must at least stop what you are doing, say hello, and wait for the visitor to tell you the purpose of the visit.

If the visitor is someone who has gotten into the annoying habit of popping in for a visit too often, you must break the habit by saying something like, "I'm sorry, Al, but I don't have time to see you right now. Can you come back at (consulting your calendar) 4:30?" If you do this a few times, the person will get the idea.

If the person is not a frequent visitor or is a senior executive or someone from outside the firm, the first thing to do is to get up and come around your desk to greet him or her with a handshake. If you get a call that a visitor is in the reception area, go out and greet the person before leading the way back to your office. If there is a coat, take it and hang it up or hand it to a receptionist or an assistant to hang up. Indicate where you would like the visitor to sit, and don't return to your seat until the visitor is seated.

When You're the Visitor

As the guest, you have to be particularly sensitive about how you handle the first few minutes while visiting someone else's office.

If you are visiting a colleague, remember that no matter how friendly the two of you are, you are still a guest. Don't enter if you can see that he or she is on the telephone or with someone. If your colleague is alone, ask if he or she is free at the moment. If it's going to be a short visit, don't sit down. If it's going to be a longer visit, say so: "Do you have time to go over that Benson matter? I want to be sure we're both on the same page before we go into the meeting."

Never touch anything on someone else's desk. Don't even turn a family picture around so that you can have a better look at it.

Here are some general guidelines to keep in mind when visiting someone's office:

- If you have a coat, ask where you can hang it. If there is no place to hang it, drape it over a chair. Don't carry it around.
- If you are late, apologize and explain.
- Wait to be told where to sit. If the host does not tell you where to sit and remains seated, don't remain standing. You are not in the principal's office. Take what seems to be the most appropriate chair.
- Don't talk to the top of the person's head. Wait for him to look at you before you speak.
- Don't spread out. Keep papers or documents on your lap, not on someone else's desk or the floor. Put your briefcase and/or handbag on the floor beside you.

Going Up in Smoke

A smoker's life is not an easy one in today's business world. Tobacco use can cause an otherwise excellent first impression to go up in smoke. Because of the now-documented threat of secondhand smoke, some nonsmokers consider the presence of tobacco smoke in the air an actual assault on their health, so smokers are now often met with belligerent reactions.

Once a symbol of sophistication, smoking now symbolizes addiction and weakness. If for any reason your building is a nonsmoking building and you are one of the smokers who stand outside the entrance to smoke, be aware that you are apt to be stigmatized in the minds of some of those passing you on the way in and the way out.

Even if smoking is permitted in your workplace, smoke only in designated areas, and never smoke in a room where there are no ashtrays. You can smoke in your own office if company policy permits, but remember that the smell will linger there and can be offensive to visitors.

Don't say: "Do you mind if I smoke?" The other person may feel constrained to say he doesn't mind and yet still be secretly resentful. If there is any doubt whatsoever, don't ask and don't smoke.

At lunch, even in a smoking section, it's best to refrain. If you must light up, wait until after everyone has finished eating. Never use a plate or saucer as an ashtray.

Don't Dally with Doors

Some people think that doors present an opportunity to demonstrate that they have good manners. They dash ahead of others so that they can open the door. They stand there holding the door open for someone, even if that person is a good distance away.

Uncertainty about doors so often causes people to create an unfavorable first impression, and it is so unnecessary. Just remember that there is one main rule: Regardless of gender, if you are the first of a group to reach the door, open it and go through it, holding it long enough to make sure it doesn't slam into the person following you. If you are alone, it is a good idea to look over your shoulder to make sure no one will be hit when you release the door.

It is no longer necessary for men to hold doors open for women to pass through just because they are women. In fact, women sometimes resent such practices.

If someone is coming along carrying packages or a child, wait and hold the door open for that person.

In the company of someone like a senior executive or an honored guest, it is a good idea to allow that person to reach the door and go through it first.

All of these rules and suggestions are set aside when you are hosting others. In this case, it's a good idea to open the door for your guests and motion them to precede you. If it's a revolving door, you go through first and wait for the others on the opposite side.

Always thank a person who holds the door for you, even if you wish he or she hadn't.

Elevator Letdowns

A lot of unnecessary and nonsensical dodging and dancing goes on in the name of politeness when it comes to elevators. Don't let uncertainty about elevator etiquette create a negative impression. As with doors, there is one basic rule: Do not maneuver around so that someone else can be the first one on or off.

If you are among the first to enter on the ground floor and you are getting off at a lower floor, stand in the corner near the door so that others can fill in the space behind you. If you are in the front and are getting off at a higher floor, step out, keep your hand on the door to prevent it from closing, and let people exit before reboarding.

If there are others getting aboard behind you, press the hold button to keep the doors open until everyone is inside. If you are at the control panel, ask people to call out their floors and press the buttons for them.

People should not remove hats, coats, or gloves while in an elevator with others because you are apt to bump or annoy other passengers.

Presents Presence

People's perceptions of how you present yourself can be changed radically by the way you present gifts. Gift-giving is an area in which care and caution must be exercised.

Rule number one is: Extravagance is bad manners and bad strategy.

If you are giving gifts to employees at holidays or on other special occasions, remember that you are setting a benchmark. Employees might expect the value of this year's gift to be matched or exceeded in future years. A substantial gift one year followed by a token gift the next year can cause disappointment and confusion, or it can start a rumor that the company is experiencing hard times.

A twenty-five-dollar ceiling is a good guideline. This is the limit the government puts on such expenditures in order for them to be tax deductible. There are exceptions, of course. If the employee has been with the company for a long time or if a personal relationship exists, as it sometimes does with executive assistants, you might want to spend up to $100, but no more. It's a good idea to keep a record of who gets what and when.

Whatever the boss does, the employee is under no obligation to give gifts to superiors, and in fact it might even be a very bad idea. There is always the danger of being accused of apple-polishing.

The best time to give a gift to the boss is when something good and, perhaps, unexpected happens. Then it should take the form of some cookies or brownies or a bouquet of flowers from your garden.

Whoever the recipient is, he or she should be made to feel that some thought went into the selection of the gift. This might involve calling someone's secretary or spouse to inquire about hobbies or favorite music, books, or food.

In any case, gifts should be wrapped nicely and presented in person, whenever possible. A handwritten note, even if it is just a few words, is immeasurably better than a gift-shop card with printed platitudes.

You are, in essence, presenting yourself when you present a gift, and you can create an immediate negative impression by making one of the more common gift-giving mistakes. Here are some rules regarding gifts:

- Never send a joke gift. Such gifts are funny for only a moment, and often not even that long.
- Never send a gift of alcohol to a person's office. Most companies prohibit alcohol consumption on the job, and the mere presence of a bottle of booze on somebody's desk is unprofessional.
- Never send a gift to the office of a newspaper reporter or editor to thank him or her for good publicity. It looks too much like a payoff and will embarrass the person in front of their colleagues.
- Be careful about gifts of flowers. Particularly red roses may be construed as having romantic implications. Green plants are safer.

Receive every gift graciously. Whatever it is, however inappropriate it may seem, it represents some thought and effort on the part of the giver. Respond to that thought and effort even if you can't muster any enthusiasm for the gift itself.

Don't let familiarity or the dulling effect of routine cause you to squander whatever advantages you earned by making a good first impression. Keep making that good impression over and over.

The most important things to remember about everyday office etiquette are:

- Keep a little space in your relationships. Rules and roles change, and you must have the flexibility to change with them. Remember that your peer today may be your superior or subordinate or client by tomorrow.
- The tone and style of the workplace is set by top management. Take your cue from them.
- Treat everyone with respect and kindness.
- Let relationships evolve naturally.
- Respect people's space.

9

Conversation Is Not Small Talk

Cocktails. Regional reps. Some clients. Colleagues, bosses, and strangers.

George Rogers enters the room reluctantly. He has decided he is not good at what he calls "chit chat" and dreads occasions such as this.

He heads right for the bar, but he is neatly intercepted by Linda Bains, the new honcho in Human Resources. Linda says, "George, I'd like to introduce Gail Greenberg. She just joined our San Diego office."

"Oh, hi, Gail. Nice to meet you," George replies.

Gail smiles, shakes hands, says nothing. Linda Bains drifts away.

George says, "You, ah, you from San Diego originally?"

"No, I'm not," states Gail.

"Oh." Silence. George, desperate for something to say, tries: "I'm from right here in New York."

"Really?"

"Yeah. Grew up in Queens, actually."

"I see."

Silence. With desperation threatening to escalate into panic, George falls back on something he feels comfortable with. He begins telling her about his position with the company. After a few minutes, Gail excuses herself in the middle of one of George's sentences and walks away.

"I hate these things," George thinks as he gloomily resumes his trek to the bar.

Nothing Small About It

George thinks the reason he is not good at small talk is because he is a serious person. He is seriously mistaken. The real reason is that he hasn't armed himself with the skills and the techniques that make casual conversation easy, pleasant, and rewarding.

Those who know how to make a good first impression at parties, social events, or even business functions know that there is nothing small about small talk. What they might NOT know is that it is easy to get better at it, and it is within the capacity of everyone to become good at it. It's what the experts call "learned behavior."

First, let's examine what happens in the first few seconds: The conversation will ordinarily begin in one of three ways.

1. You will approach someone.
2. Someone will approach you.
3. Someone will introduce you.

In the *first* instance, make sure they see you coming. Try to avoid a rear or side approach that requires a tap on the shoulder or the charade of clearing your throat to get attention.

When the other person sees you, say his name if you know it. If not, smile, put out your hand and say: "Hello, I'm George Rogers."

(TIP: If you are at a party, it's a good idea to carry your drink in your *left* hand to avoid greeting people with a cold, damp handshake.)

Make eye contact, and be sure your handshake is firm but not hard. (See the section on handshakes in Chapter 3.)

In addition to your name, provide a nugget of information to give the other person a handle on who you are: "Hello. I'm George Rogers, Troy Gallagher's partner."

The *second* way in which a conversation begins is when someone approaches you. When that happens, give the other person your full attention immediately. Pay particular attention to the person's name—say it silently to yourself right away, and use it in the conversation as soon as you can. Listen for any nugget of information that can serve as the basis for launching a conversation.

The *third* way in which a conversation gets launched is when you are being introduced to someone. When that happens, look first at the introducer and then at the person you are meeting. Again, listen carefully. Those first few words are crucial. (See the section on greeting in Chapter 3.)

The moment of introduction is the moment when you stop thinking about yourself, your appearance, and what you are hoping to accomplish at this gathering. It is the moment when you begin focusing on the other person.

If you are engaged in conversation with one or more people and a new person joins you, you can say: "We were just talking about problems getting to and from airports these days, especially in the big cities." If you are the new person, ask what the topic of conversation is and join in when an opportunity presents itself.

Listen Here

Remember that when people describe someone as "a good conversationalist," they really mean "a good listener."

Although it is important to listen carefully, it is also important to *look* as if you are listening carefully. You do that by an occasional nod, by leaning forward slightly when the other person speaks, by saying "yes" or "I see" when appropriate, and by looking at the speaker. You might want to use the "Cyclops" technique: Instead of locking onto the other person's eyeballs, focus on the spot between his or her eyebrows. (There is also a theory that says you can direct your gaze anywhere from the hairline to the chin. Find out what works best for you.)

Your main job is to get the other person to talk. You do this by asking questions and following up on any information you are given.

Let's give George Rogers another chance at meeting and impressing Gail Greenberg. Human Resources' Linda Bains says, "George, I'd like to introduce Gail Greenberg. She just joined our San Diego office."

The only nugget of information at his disposal is the San Diego connection.

He almost says, "I was in San Diego last June. Went to the famous San Diego Zoo."

This would virtually force Gail to say, "Oh, what did you think of it?"

And he would soon find that they were talking about Rogers, not Greenberg. Instead, he directs the topic back to her: "San Diego has a lot more going for it than most cities. How do you like living there?"

In her response, he listens for further opportunities to ask Greenberg about herself and her experiences—where she lived before San Diego, what she likes and hates most about the city or the West Coast in general, how life there compares or contrasts with life in New York, or the East, or wherever she lived previously.

Golden Cliches

Don't worry about sounding a bit trite. It is perfectly okay to use certain cliches to get a conversation going. After all, they got to be cliches because they have proven over the years to be effective. Even the weather can be a useful conversation starter.

George: "I imagine the weather there is quite a bit different from what we're going through here in New York."

Gail: "It sure is, but I don't mind this kind of weather, I grew up in Minnesota."

Now, George can ask about Minnesota or a Midwest childhood, how she got to San Diego, and what brings her to New York.

You can use mutual acquaintances—West Coast colleagues she might know or, better still, the person who introduced you.

George: "How do you know Linda Bains?"

Gail: "We met at that Chicago seminar on liability insurance legislation."

This allows George to follow up with "I was sorry to miss that. Was it interesting?" or "Did you get to see much of Chicago?"

Try to ask open-ended questions, as opposed to those that can be answered with a simple yes or no, answers that erect stop signs on the conversational highway. For example, "How often do you get to New York?" is better than "Is this your first visit to New York?"

Another useful conversational cliche is the news. People like being asked what they think about current events: "Did you feel any effects of the big earthquake in the north?"

True Confessions

Another tactic is to confess, after the conversation gets rolling, to being a bit uncomfortable: "I find big parties like this kind of overwhelming" or "I really enjoy meeting people, once I get over being a little shy."

Nothing encourages people to start talking like a desire to get other people to start talking.

Every conversational topic flowers and dies naturally. If the talk about airline travel, for example, is brisk and interesting, relax and enjoy it. When it begins to wither, try changing the topic. The easiest way is to switch to a related topic:

"Speaking of traveling, have you noticed that corporate hotel rates have been going up almost everywhere?"

What You Don't Say

What you don't say can be almost as important as what you do say. At a party, it's a good idea to stay away from anything as grim as airplane crashes and such heavily mined battle-fields as religion and sex.

It is impossible, however, to avoid all controversial subjects. If you find that you disagree with what the other person is saying, it is perfectly okay to disagree. When the other person has stated his position, you can respond with your own, without seeming to pass judgment on his: "Another way of looking at it is . . ." or "I tend to side with those who think . . ." But you should not make a critical remark like "You're wrong about that."

Lighten Up

Nothing destroys a convivial conversation like someone who is trying too hard. You will know that you are trying too hard if:

- You find yourself waiting for a conversational pause so you can jump in with your next prepared statement or question.

- If you are "speed-talking." Talking too fast gives the impression that you are afraid somebody will interrupt you before you finish expressing your thought. (Conversely, you will know that you are "slow-talking" if people start finishing your sentences for you or nodding agreement before you have even reached your point.)

Here are some other conversational DOs and DON'Ts:

- Don't tell a joke that lasts longer that 30 seconds or that is even slightly off-color or involves race or ethnicity.
- Don't talk about your health, your recent promotion, or the cost of things these days. Avoid religion and politics.
- Don't watch other people moving around the room while someone is talking to you.
- Do stand upright, but not at attention.
- Don't fold your arms. It's distracting.
- Do keep your hands away from your face.
- Don't shift your weight around as if you're preparing to return a tennis serve.

Breaking Away

Ending a conversation can be every bit as important as getting one started. The experts tell us that we require both acknowledgment and closure from others. The need for *acknowledgment* is the reason we are so annoyed when the receptionist says "Please hold" and cuts us off before we can respond, and the reason we are less annoyed waiting in line when the clerk says "I'll be right with you." The need for *closure* engenders the same feelings when someone abruptly departs without a word or drifts away without some indication that a conversation has occurred.

When you sense that a conversation has run its course or you find that it is necessary for you to move on, make your getaway with as much grace as possible. Wait for a break in the conversation, and then say something like the following:

- "I'm going to replenish my drink." (Make sure you are not carrying a full glass when you say this.)
- "Well, I've got to say hello to . . ."
- "That food looks delicious. I think I'll have some . . ."

Follow that up with: "It was good talking with you. I enjoyed hearing about life on your sunny coast."

If others have joined you and another conversation has started up, it is still necessary to make some sort of parting gesture, even if it is only eye contact and a wave.

⊞

If I had to choose only one thing that every reader would learn from this chapter, it would be the fact that worries about your own ability to engage in casual conversation comfortably and successfully tend to disappear when you focus on the other person and concentrate on keeping the conversation flowing.

10

Secrets of the Public Speakers

Many of the techniques covered in Chapter 9 concerning making a good first and lasting impression during conversation also apply to speaking to more than one person— whether it's a few colleagues at a small dinner party or an auditorium full of people. First impressions are never more important than in these situations. And as always, the first impressions you make depend heavily on your advance preparations.

As with so-called small talk, being good at public speaking is a learned behavior. Saying you suffer from stage fright is no excuse. Everybody does, and anybody can get over it.

To begin with, it helps to know that the elevated blood pressure, the tremble in the fingers, and the quickened heartbeat are reactions common to all humans, and one that was shared by Brother Orf, your cave-dwelling ancestor. When Orf heard the throaty rumble of a jungle beast, adrenaline was pumped into his bloodstream, and his body got ready to scamper up a tree, or if absolutely necessary engage in combat. Experts call it the flight-or-fight reaction.

What Orf didn't know is that there are mental and physical tricks that can be used to control this reaction.

Because your stage fright is a right-brain function, instinctive and emotional, try to counter it with left-brain activity. You can think about how your talk is organized or run over the principal points you want to make. Or you can just do a math problem in your head or simply count—backward or forward.

And you can instruct your left brain to tell old Orf that the audience is not a saber-toothed tiger looking for lunch. The audience wants to like you. They want to relax and have a pleasant experience almost as much as you do. They are on your side.

Breathe. Inhale deeply through your nostrils and exhale through your mouth. It works.

Smile. It will help to relax both you and the audience.

Some people find that it helps them to deliver the speech in advance to a friend. Others like to record the speech in private so that they can listen to it. I usually record the entire speech and play it while I'm driving.

The Four Questions

I spend a lot of time talking to groups, from a handful of school children to a board of directors to hundreds in an auditorium or thousands in a television audience. Before each and every event, I take some time to ask myself the same four questions:

1. *Who do they think I am?* This involves thinking about what relationship you have, if any, with your audience and how you would like them to perceive you.

2. *What do I want to accomplish?* Focus on your objective. Maybe you are going to ask for a raise, explain a situation, praise another person or some project or institution. Maybe your mission is to welcome, to instruct, to motivate, to persuade.

3. *To whom am I talking?* Think about why the others (the audience) are there and what might be their possible points of view concerning you and your topic. What are their expectations, and what are their shared characteristics?

4. *Where am I?* Find out ahead of time about the physical space. It will determine how you use your voice and gestures, whether you will need a microphone, whether you will be standing or sitting. (Stand whenever you have a choice.) Check out the audiovisual equipment, and find out who will be operating it. Think about what you will do when the equipment breaks down. (Assume that it will.)

If you have considered all of these things, if you are sure you are well groomed and dressed appropriately, if you are confident of your grasp of your material, if you have convinced yourself that the audience wants to like you—then you have a very good chance of making an excellent first impression.

The Big Beginning

The beginning of your remarks can reinforce the preparation you have made for any speaking event.

First, make sure you have the first few words and the first few ideas firmly in mind. You may want to begin by introducing yourself, even if somebody has already introduced you. If possible, mention something that connects you with the audience as part of your self-introduction: "Like most of you, I have been working in the field of electronics for quite some time."

Some speakers open by complimenting the audience, making some startling or provocative statement, quoting a prominent or historical person, or telling a joke or an anecdote.

The absolutely unbreakable rules for using a joke or an anecdote are that they must not be vulgar or offensive, they must be brief, and they must have a direct connection with the audience or the subject of your talk. (Books with useful jokes and anecdotes can be found in libraries and the larger bookstores, generally in a section called "public speaking.")

Adjust your language to your audience. You wouldn't use the same language with scientists as you would with artists. The danger here is talking down. Because those in the audience are young or unfamiliar with the topic doesn't mean that they are slow or need long explanations or lots of repetition. However, with children, you will want to spice up your presentation with gestures, vivid images, and jokes because their attention span is shorter than that of most adults.

Some Basics

Having decided which points you want to make, remember a couple of rules of thumb: It is unwise to try to make more than four major points in a twenty-minute speech. The usual technique is to make your point, provide some sort of descriptive example, and then make the same point again.

Keep your head up, speak clearly, and control the volume of your voice and the pace of your words. Inexperienced speakers tend to get louder as they go along, until the audience begins to think it is being addressed by a sideshow barker. Think in terms of projecting rather than loudness. Inexperienced speakers also have a tendency to speak quickly, as if every moment must be filled with as much information as possible.

The Big Closing

A good closing is essential. Lapses and even tedious material in the body of the speech will be forgiven or forgotten if the closing is strong and satisfying. (One thing that will not be forgiven is exceeding your allotted time. Stop when your time is up, even if you have not covered all of the material you had planned to cover. Remember that the audience doesn't know you wanted to say more.)

If your talk has been light, save your best joke for the end, or put some humorous spin on the material already presented.

If your talk has been of the "call to action" variety, don't be afraid to trot out some dramatic or emotional language at the end. You don't have to create original material for this purpose. Quote a portion of some great speech or a few lines of stirring poetry. (It's a good idea to have a few of these arrows in your quiver at all times. Excellent sources for this material are *Bartlett's Familiar Quotations* and *The Oxford Book of Quotations.*)

When you have finished, just say thank you and sit down. Don't wave or otherwise acknowledge applause (or any other expression of approval or disapproval on the part of the audience).

If there is to be a question-and-answer session, say so. Raise your hand briefly to indicate the protocol to be followed by questioners. Don't say, "Good question." It implies you are judging or comparing the quality of questions. Don't address the questioner by name unless you are prepared to call everyone in the room by name.

So, don't let the prospect of speaking before a group of people dismay you. Expect some stage fright. It's normal, and it can be handled. Be prepared. Remember that the key idea is that *you* are more important than the material. The listeners want to hear what *you* have to say and how *you* present the material.

11

Correspondence

A person I had never met before wrote to me asking if there was a job for him with my company. Before I even read his correspondence, I knew that there was not and never would be. His query was typed on a postcard, signed in apparent haste with a ballpoint pen.

A few days later, I received a letter from another stranger. This person was not seeking a job, but a small favor. The letter was neatly written on good paper with a fountain pen, properly addressed and politely worded.

My favorable impression of the second correspondent was formed even before I opened the attractive, neatly and correctly addressed envelope. I was happy to do as the writer asked.

So often, the first impression someone has of us is through correspondence, and it is important for us to realize that in many ways, the pen is mightier than the computer—not to mention the telephone.

A letter, gracefully written on good stationery, has power no e-mail message or computer printout can equal. It has substance beyond its message. It can be put away and reread later. It can be shown to others. A letter can be a double gift, pleasing the sender as well as the receiver.

In many ways, you will be fortunate if someone who is important to you receives his or her first impression of you in the form of a letter—you will have had time to think about how you wish to present yourself, and the recipient will be able to receive your message without such distractions as appearance, voice, and dress.

Even those you have met previously will receive a new "first impression" of you when they first receive written correspondence from you.

Let's deal first with how a letter should look and some of the qualities common to all good letters.

A Matter of Style

The highest virtues of any letter are clarity and sincerity. Your letter will be more clear if you have a definite idea of what you are going to say before you begin writing. To this end, a rough outline is recommended, followed by a draft of the letter.

Simple language will not make you appear to be simple-minded. Showing off—by using big words or obscure references and images—is nowhere more obvious and more irritating than in a letter. Real situations and real feelings can be described very well without extravagant language. Literature, both classical and contemporary, abound with examples.

When someone says, "I never know what to say," they really mean, "I don't know how to approach this thing." Every writer knows that the best way to get unblocked is to start writing. Get a piece of scrap paper and begin a draft. Get the words flowing, even the wrong words, and the right words will follow.

Greeting

In salutations, use first names for informal letters to people you already know. Use an honorific and last name for others.

Body

A good way to start the body of a letter is by mentioning past correspondence or the most recent meeting you had with the other person. Good news is always a good beginning, "You will be pleased to hear that . . ." If you refer to past correspondence, never begin by apologizing for not writing sooner. You can say something like, "You have been in my thoughts a great deal since I received your last letter, and I'm finally getting around to responding." The word "you" is always a better beginning than the word "I."

As for the rest of the letter, remember that letters are supposed to convey news. Talk about what has been happening with you and with mutual friends.

You can end with a hope that you will be seeing the recipient soon and that the letter finds him or her well. You can also ask that your best wishes be passed along to mutual friends.

Ending

The most formal letters require "Sincerely." Other endings, from formal to familiar, are "Yours truly," "Regards," "Best wishes," "Affectionately," and "Love."

111

Love is a wonderful thing, but it may not be quite right, even for an affectionate letter. If so, try "Fondly." If you want to step back even a bit further, there's always "As ever" or "As always."

"Cordially" is perhaps out of date, but I like it because it is correct and, I think, warmer than "Sincerely."

"Gratefully" is great for letters of thanks, and "Respectfully" and "Respectfully yours" are reserved for closing a letter to the clergy.

Structuring Your Letter

Here are the general rules governing the appearance of your letter.

- Begin by writing your address in the upper right corner, unless, of course, the address is printed at the top of the page. You can skip the return address if you are sure the recipient knows perfectly well where you live.
- The date goes under the address or at the bottom left corner of the letter. Always write out the month instead of using numerals.
- The salutation goes flush left.
- Leave a line of space and indent before beginning the body of the letter.

With a folded-over letter sheet, begin writing on the first page and go to page three if needed, skipping page two. If you know the letter will run longer than two pages, go with the usual sequence: 1,2,3,4.

Fountain pens make letters look so much better than ballpoints. They communicate authority. A good fountain pen is certainly worth the investment. It is the sort of detail that gets noticed. Colored inks are okay for casual notes, but always use black ink for a condolence letter or when replying to a formal invitation.

Figure 1 shows a sample letter on letterhead.

Grammar

Errors in grammar, spelling, and punctuation can ruin your letter. These errors like to lurk in long, complicated sentences. Simple, direct sentences are not only safer, they are stylistically superior.

A few of the errors I see most often include using "less," which denotes quantities such as water, when you mean "fewer," which denotes a number of things you can count—you have *less* water and *fewer* bricks.

"Between you and I" might sound correct, but it should be "between you and me"—*me* is the object of the preposition *between*. Do not use "irregardless"; instead use "regardless."

Do not use an adverb with verbs like *feel, taste,* or *look*—"feel badly" literally means "a flawed sense of touch."

Use apostrophies to represent a missing letter and not to make a word plural. "It's" means "it is," and "its" is the possessive of "it"—*it's* a good idea to keep the book with *its* jacket.

Do not use phrases like "I, myself," "he, himself," or "you, yourself"—they are redundant. "I think that the contract is a good one" is strong enough, you do not need, "I, myself, think . . ."

113

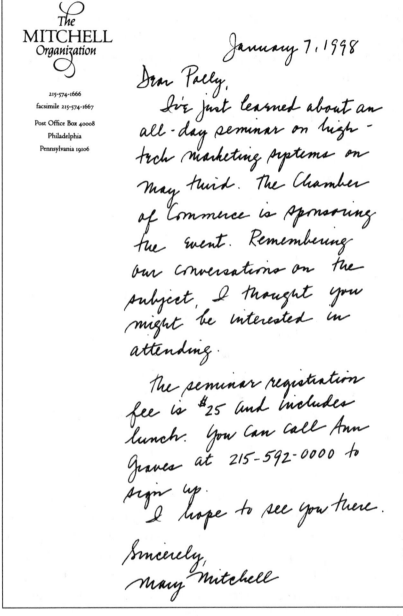

Figure 1. A letter conveying information.

Perhaps the most common grammatical error is failing to have the number of the noun agree with the verb—"A group *is* (not *are*) waiting"; "Everyone *is* eligible." "Either Mike or Carmen *is* going to attend the conference"; "Both Mike and Carmen *are* qualified to represent the company."

The most common punctuation error is not putting a comma before the conjunction in a compound sentence, which is two complete sentences connected by "and" or "but" or another conjunction. Again, keeping the style simple helps us to avoid punctuation errors. Long sentences, requiring lots of hyphens and semicolons, are apt to get you into punctuation purgatory.

Types of Letters

Here are the types of letters people are most called upon to write:

Thank You Note

Here is my foolproof, tried-and-true, three-step formula for writing thank you letters that don't feel or read like boring "duty" scratchings.

1. Thank the person for the specific gift, mentioning the gift by name.
2. Acknowledge the effort that went into choosing, purchasing, wrapping, or, if such is the case, making the gift.

3. Report how you have used or will use the gift.

See Figures 2, 3, and 4 for examples of different types of thank-you notes.

If you know the person well, signing just your first name would be sufficient.

Even if you thanked someone in person, it is important to follow up with a note.

When thanking someone for a gift of money, don't mention the amount. The phrase "your generous gift" will do.

When refusing a gift, your note should say that you don't feel you can accept the gift but should thank the person for "your thoughtfulness."

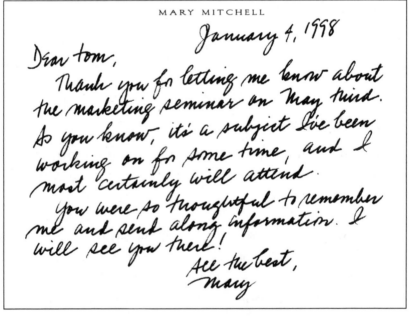

Figure 2. A thank-you note for a courtesy. It is shown on a classic correspondence card with the name engraved.

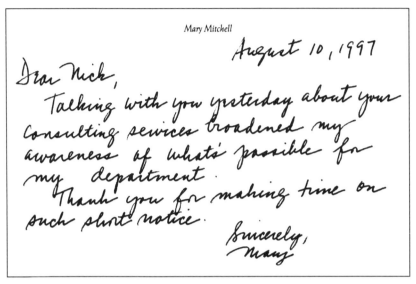

Figure 3. A thank-you note for a service. It is written on another, slightly different style of correspondence card.

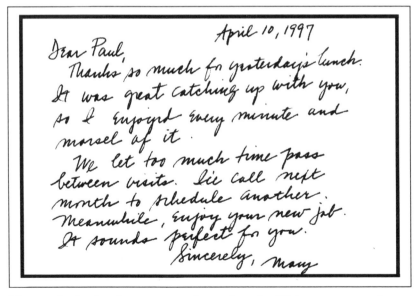

Figure 4. A thank-you note for a lunch. This correspondence card has dark borders but no name engraved on it.

No, a printed thank you card or a note from a gift shop is not acceptable.

No, a telephone call will not do.

Condolence Letter

When tragedy overtakes a colleague or a friend, a letter of condolence is called for. There is no need to face this task with dread. Plan your letter based on the idea that a condolence letter should do three things for the recipient:

1. It should acknowledge their loss and their suffering, and it should let them know that you sympathize with their bereavement.
2. It should convey a sincere desire to help in some way.
3. If there has been a death, the letter should praise the character, the accomplishments, and the devotion of the deceased.

See Figure 5 for a sample condolence letter.

Avoid stressing how sad you feel. The letter is supposed to comfort others, not make them feel sorry for you.

A condolence letter often will be saved and become a part of the family archives. Therefore, although it should be personal, it should also be somewhat formal.

Other Kinds of Letters

Letters of congratulations also may be kept for years. However, the tone is quite informal, even breezy. They must mention the reason for the congratulations and say that the happy recipient deserved whatever it was.

MARY MITCHELL

July 10th

Dear Mrs. Clancy,

Please accept my deepest sympathy on the loss of your husband, Michael. His passing was a great blow to all of us, and I know that no words of mine can ease your grief.

Michael was my first supervisor when I came to work at Filbert's. His kindness and guidance

2

helped me get started there. His ability, together with his fine sense of humor, made him the most popular "boss" in the company. We will all miss him.

You probably know that I live just a few blocks away.

Figure 5. A note of condolence. It is written on a letter sheet, the most formal personal stationery. If the note is to be longer than 2 pages, the pages should be used in order, as if you were writing in a book.

119

3

I hope you'll call if there is anything I can do to help you or your family in the sad, difficult days ahead. In a couple weeks I'll call to see if you need anything — walk the dog, grocery shopping, whatever.

Sincerely,

Mary

Figure 5. (*Continued*)

Dear John:

My heartiest congratulations on receiving a Nieman Fellowship. It is a very high honor, and you richly deserve it in light of your tenacious reporting and fine writing. Harvard will be a better place for your presence.

Best,

Anna Murphy

If you have offended someone, apologize in person, if possible, and follow it up with a letter. The letter must say clearly and humbly that you are sorry. If there is any way to make amends, promise to do so in the letter.

Dear Andy:

I am terribly sorry for knocking over your beautiful Chinese vase. It was clumsy of me, and I want to offer you my profound apologies. Be assured that I will replace the vase as soon as possible.

Sincerely,

Judith Dorne

For a sample of an invitation to a business party, see Figure 6.

Casual Notes

It may be that some people will get their first impression of your personality through a note, rather than a letter. In any case, a note is not something to be dashed off carelessly, even though it is brief and probably will be more casual than a letter.

If you have a choice between sending a note and picking up the telephone, the inherent advantages of writing a note should be considered.

Too often, telephone calls don't come off the way you plan. The other person speaks before you can deliver the lit-

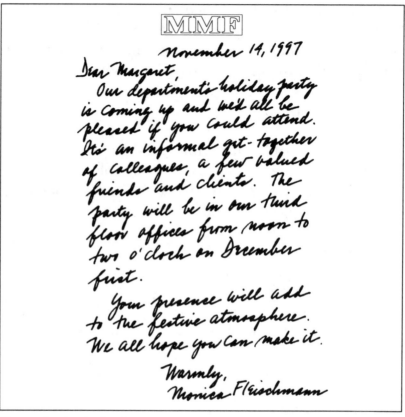

Figure 6. An invitation, shown on a half sheet.

tle speech you had in mind. The mood shifts. The prepared phrases are no longer appropriate.

A note, on the other hand, can do just exactly what you want it to do. It doesn't have to be lyrical.

> Dear Joan,
> We haven't talked in ages. Let's have lunch next week.

It doesn't have to be long.

Dear Hank,
Don't forget to call our pal Martha.

It doesn't even have to be original.

Dear Dylan,
It was great seeing you on Thursday. You haven't changed a bit.

Always,

Saul

Think first about your "root" message, and get to it promptly. Consider your relationship with the recipient. Is it a close friend, your boss, somebody you would like to know better?

Once again, people have trouble getting started. If you are stuck, try one of these perennials:

"I was thinking (or remembering) . . ."
"What a . . ." followed by "grand occasion," "welcome gift," "terrific surprise . . ."
"I can't tell you how much . . ."

If you come up with a good, all-purpose opening, write it down for future reference. However, all of these openings wear easily and should be used sparingly.

Sometimes, a favorite quote will send just the right message. "No wise man ever wished to be younger."—Jonathan Swift.

Stationery

Just as first impressions of us are influenced more by what people see than by what we say, so we may be judged on how our letters and other correspondence *look*. It is a case where the medium is a crucial part of the message.

The rigid rules governing stationery in past generations have been stretched and relaxed in today's society. A major reason is the availability of computer programs for word processing and graphics that provide opportunities for expressing personal style and creativity.

However, certain basic rules remain, and it is important to know them.

Paper and Printing

You know when you are dealing with fine paper by its texture and weight. The best paper is made from unlaundered, undyed, new cotton rag. Cheaper paper is made from vegetable fibers, sometimes combined with wood pulp. In all cases, the higher the rag content, the better the paper. (Rag content is often noted on stationery boxes.)

Watermarks are another indication of good stationery. Watermarks are revealed when you hold the paper up to the light. Genuine watermarks of legitimate manufacturers look slightly blurred. Artificial watermarks usually are betrayed by their sharpness.

Engraving is the highest quality printing. The symbols are etched into a metal plate and then stamped onto paper in a press. You can tell real engraving by the raised, embossed quality. Turn the paper over and see that the paper is slightly indented.

Decide on whether you want your stationery engraved or simply printed. Avoid thermography—a process that seeks to imitate engraving but cannot match its quality. You can spot thermography by noticing how easily the printing flakes off when you scratch it with your fingernail. Ersatz engraving, in the form of thermography, should be avoided because stationery, like people, ought not to pretend it is something it isn't.

Printing these days can produce a very good and high-quality image without involving a great deal of expense.

Personal Stationery

Most of us need three kinds of personal stationery—formal writing paper, personal business stationery, and social paper.

Formal writing paper is used for things like condolence letters or for responding to formal invitations. It should be plain white or ecru letter sheets or cards.

Personal business stationery is used for matters related to your career and for letting the store know that your dishwasher is the wrong color and size. This correspondence should be on a single sheet in a neutral color.

Social paper is used for informal invitations and replies, thank you notes, and most social correspondence. This can express your personality with colored papers, borders, and lined envelopes and may be in the form of a single sheet, a folded note, or a single card.

For a single solution to many of the above requirements, you might consider house stationery. This is usually a single sheet with your address at the top and can be used by all members of the household.

■■

You may not need custom-printed or engraved stationery. Stationery stores, department stores, and some jewelers carry plain stationery in all the appropriate forms. Personalizing, however, is a nice and useful luxury.

■■

The U.S. Postal Service requires that envelopes be at least 3.5 by 5 inches. The Postal Service will still deliver mail with the return address on the back, which is a long-standing formal custom. However, it is generally more convenient to put the return address on the front upper-left-hand corner for all but the most formal invitations.

Women

Once, every well-bred woman used only fold-over notes rather than flat stationery. Women can now select stationery that complements their handwriting, style, and tastes. Some find that large, letter-size sheets accommodate their large-script flair. However, it is still a good idea to avoid wild ink colors in favor of more multiuseful, conservative ones such as black, blue, or gray.

On calling cards, a woman has the option of which title or honorific to use. A married woman may use Mrs. Daniel Fleischmann or the more contemporary Ms. Mary Fleischmann. It is unnecessary and perhaps a bit pretentious (but not incorrect) for a single woman to use "Miss" before her name, although using Ms. is fine.

When a person has a Ph.D., only use that within professional context; not socially. Thus, Joan Carson, Ph.D., Department of English, The College of New Rochelle, is correct. The salutation on the letter then would read, "Dear Dr. Carson."

If you use different names in different situations—say, your maiden name for business and your married name socially—it would be more practical to have your stationery printed with the address only. A medical doctor may use Dr. before her name. A woman in the military or the clergy may also use a title.

Women use a title only on calling cards (gift enclosures), never on a sheet or a note or a correspondence card. The same is true for men.

Men

A man's name should appear without title on his stationery unless he happens to be a medical doctor, in which case Dr. may be used. (M.D. is used only professionally.) A man will also use a title if he is a clergyman or a member of the military.

Both

Another very useful piece of stationery is the correspondence card. It may, in fact, be the most used item of stationery in some business people's arsenal. Mine are single cards, about 6 by 4 inches. They can be colored or simply have a colored border. They can be plain or engraved with your name or monogram. They may be used for any kind of short note, including thank you notes. They may also be used for sending or for replying to informal invitations.

Monograms

If you are going to monogram your stationery, it is best to use three initials. If, however, your name is Ann Sterling Smith, you will be better off using two initials. A single initial leaves too many unanswered questions. You can buy preprinted notes with single initials, but they seem to me to be useless and silly.

Monograms are either three initials set in consecutive order or three initials with the initial of the last name in larger size in the middle of the other two. Monograms should be centered at the top of the page or, on a folded note, centered on the front or in the upper left corner.

A single woman or a married woman who retains her maiden name uses the initials of her first, middle, and last names. A married woman who uses her husband's name uses the initials of her first name, her maiden name and her married name.

A Coat of Arms

Knights wore special colors and insignia on jackets worn over their armor so that they could get full credit for heroic deeds in battle or in tournaments. The heralds who kept score at the tournaments kept records of the various colors and insignia, thus the term *heraldry*.

Direct male descendants inherit the family coat of arms, as do daughters if there are no male heirs. When such a woman marries a man who does not have a coat of arms, she does not use her coat of arms after her marriage.

Because so many upstarts were using coats of arms illegitimately, the College of Arms was chartered in 1484 to regulate heraldry, as it continues to do today. In America, the New England Historic Genealogical Society in Boston will rule on whether your family is entitled to "bear arms." It is a privilege that cannot be awarded. It must be inherited.

If you have a coat of arms, it may be used on personal stationery and invitations, preferably embossed without color.

Mastering the techniques and observing the traditional rules of written communications can put you at ease with a pen in your hand. And, let's face it, nothing quite replaces the handwritten letter or note. If your penmanship truly does resemble Chinese algebra, you may be better off typing your messages. But it's never the same.

12

Electronic Etiquette

The house across the street came on the market, and it occurred to me that it might be what my husband Danny and I were looking for. I called the real estate agent and listened to a taped message: "We're not here right now, so leave your name and number after the beep."

The speaker did not identify herself or suggest a better time to call. The message was brief, which is good voice-mail manners, but it was curt and incomplete, which is not good manners.

I left a message that said my husband and I would like to see the house. Because of our work schedules, we could only do it at 9 A.M., any weekday. I asked the agent to pick a day. I would call back to confirm, and we would meet her at the house.

Her return message came a few days later. She gave her telephone number, which I already had, said "Call me," and hung up.

I was so offended by her lack of electronic manners that I never called back. Talk about a bad first few minutes! At this writing, eight months later, the house is still for sale.

■■

Every day, it becomes more and more likely that someone's first impression of you will be received electronically. It seems as if there's a cell phone in every purse, a fax machine at every bus stop, and a computer in every playpen. Is there no limit to the electronic wizardry all around us? Is e-mail putting the Postal Service out of business?

The first impression you make in the electronic world is every bit as important as the one you make in person. It is just as easy electronically as it is in person to impress someone favorably or to convince them that you are not worth their time.

And it is not only clients and colleagues who will be judging you on the basis of your knowledge of electronic etiquette. A study released in May of 1997 by the American Management Association shows that 10.4 percent of employers tape and review telephone conversations and that 15 percent store and review e-mail.

E-mail is not the only means of committing electronic self-destruction with your trusty personal computer (PC). But before dealing with the very fundamental and specific rules for behavior that will keep you from being branded a cyberslob, let's spend a little time talking about that old friend and potential enemy, the telephone.

The Ubiquitous Phone

It is estimated that 70 percent of business is still being done over the telephone, but it is amazing how many people just don't know how to use the telephone to their advantage.

Caller Precedence

The most common error is forgetting that a speaking person almost always has precedence over a ringing telephone. If the telephone rings during a conversation, have somebody or some machine take a message. If that's not possible, apologize for the interruption to the person with whom you are speaking, answer the telephone, and tell the caller you are busy and will call back. (Be sure to keep your word to the second caller, and get back to him or her as quickly as possible. Better still, ask the caller for a convenient time to call and do your best to accommodate.)

Speaking Clearly

Another common error is speaking carelessly. Vocal quality counts for 70 percent of the impression you make during a telephone conversation. Think about your tone of voice. The other person should not have to work hard to hear and understand what you are saying.

At your desk, pick up the telephone promptly and give both your name and your department or company. Say "Hello," rather than "Hi." If the call is for someone else, say "May I tell her who's calling?" instead of simply, "Who's calling?"

When You Place a Call

If you are the one calling, nobody should have to ask "Who's calling?" Begin your call with your name and company or affiliation. After that, name the person for whom the call is intended: "Hello, this is Troy Gallagher from Microfelt, calling for Robert Jones."

This approach makes you sound confident and self-contained, and it saves time and greatly increases your chances of having your call put through promptly.

Place your own calls whenever possible. I know people who routinely hang up when a secretary says, "Please hold for Mr. Lopez." When someone has to wait for you to come on the line, the message you send is that you consider your time more important than his. The first impression in this case is entirely negative, and you begin your conversation, and perhaps your relationship with the other person, in an atmosphere of hostility.

Keep It Brief

Another common error is the Chatty Cathy syndrome. If you are friendly with the person being called, it's fine to ask how they've been or to make a reference to the last time you met. But keep it short. Have a clear idea of what you want to accomplish with the call and deal with that in a prompt and organized way.

"Hi, Donald. How have you been? It was great seeing you and Sarah at the golf outing. I'm calling about our upcoming meeting on the Greenleaf project . . ."

Getting off the point and wasting time with chatter, no matter how amiable, gives the impression that your job is of so little importance that you have time to waste and that you don't mind wasting the time of others. If you're lonesome, join a support group or take up ballroom dancing.

If you have a chatty caller on the line, it is perfectly all right to say: "We'll have to cut this short because . . ." or "I'll have to hang up now because . . ." The "because" can be things such as the fact that a meeting is about to start without you or that your lunch date has just arrived or that there's another call for which you have been waiting.

Ending a Call

How you close a telephone conversation is an important part of the other person's overall impression of the experience. Thank the other person and try to end the conversation on a positive note. Say "Goodbye." Stay away from "See ya," or "Later," or worst of all, "Bye bye." Banging the receiver down while the other person is still on the line does not give the impression of a dynamic individual working at a fast pace. The impression will be: "He said goodbye and hung up on me."

Playing Phone Tag

Sure phone tag is annoying. It's also irritating and frustrating. Someday, when everybody in the world has e-mail, the problem may go away. In the meantime, a strategy for handling telephone tag is imperative. If you make twenty calls from your desk today, there's a good chance that you will connect on the first try with only four or five of them. Accept the odds, and use some proven way of improving your chances of connecting efficiently, such as dealing cordially with the "gatekeeper."

Part of the job of a secretary or receptionist is to be a gatekeeper. If you are going to be calling a person more than once or twice, learn the name of the gatekeeper and use it. It scores points. Establishing a relationship with the gatekeeper can result in that person volunteering such information as when Ms. Feldman is apt to be free that day, when she is generally reachable, and the time time that she gets back from lunch. When you learn the best time, make it clear that you will be calling back at that time: "Fine. I'll call back a little after three and have a five-minute chat with Ms. Feldman about that warehouse in Wisconsin. I know she has been waiting to get the final word on that."

If you are asking that Ms. Feldman return your call, include the best time to reach you. Also briefly give the reason for your call, so that she can prepare a response before she picks up the phone to return your call.

Sound Advice

If you want to know how your voice sounds over the telephone, make a recording and listen to it carefully. Think of ways to improve your vocal presentation and make subsequent recordings. Using this technique, some people have found that if they smile while talking, it can be heard in their voice. Your voice can be clear without being loud or sharp. The message within your message should convey ease and confidence.

Cell Hell

Cellular telephones have provided the world with new ways to be rude. Don't whip out your cell phone for a quick call at a party, in a restaurant, on a bus, or anywhere else that is inappropriate and annoying. This means not using the phone in situations in which it would necessarily foist your half of the conversation on those around you. I, along with others in a crowded doctor's waiting room, recently had to listen to a person with a strident voice arguing with a car dealership.

And even otherwise gentle and tolerant souls think that flogging is a reasonable punishment for those (other than physicians) who bring a cell phone or a beeper to church or to the theater.

Voice Mail

Although voice mail is a convenient and useful tool, it should not end up annoying as many people as it actually does.

Once again, the message is the monster. Poorly thought out messages can be as annoying as dealing with a real, and really disagreeable, human. Think about the journalist's five W's—who, what, where, when, and why. Your message need not answer all of these questions, but generally it should not go beyond them.

If you are preparing one of those "menu" messages, remember that the perfect menu contains three choices—leave a message, call this other extension, or switch to a real human being. Add additional options only if they will save a lot of people a lot of time and effort.

Your Tape's Message
Remember that:

- Briefer is better.
- Forget about sound effects or other gimmicks. Cute is unprofessional and annoying.

137

- Write out the specific message and practice it.

The basic message should be something like: "This is Nancy Hayes of Thrift Industries speaking. Please leave a brief message with your name and telephone number. I'll call you back shortly."

If the circumstances are unusual, the message can contain more specific information:

"This is Nancy Hayes on Monday, April first. I will be traveling all day today and will not be able to return calls until after 7 P.M., New York time. Please leave your name, telephone number, and a brief message."

Leaving Messages for Others

When you find yourself leaving a message, you will make the best impression if you:

- Give your full name and affiliation.
- Say when you are calling.
- Give the specific reason for your call.
- State the best time to call you.
- Leave your complete number and pause between the area code and the rest of the number. Speak your number slowly so that the person you called can take it down without having to repeat it.

If you get a wrong number, go ahead and leave a message anyway saying you misdialed.

Speaker Phone

Avoid using the speaker whenever possible. It distorts sound and makes people feel as if they are speaking into a bull-horn. On the receiving end, the voices seem to be coming from the other end of a tunnel.

When you *do* use a speaker phone, be considerate of the person on the other end. Don't begin conversations on the speaker phone, and always ask the people with whom you are speaking for permission to put them on the speaker phone.

I recently spoke with group of people who were in a single room using a speaker phone, and it was a most uncomfortable experience. For one thing, the people in the room talked among themselves, so I never knew which remarks were directed at me. There was laughter, the point of which was unknown to me. One person left the room during the conversation without informing me, and I continued to address him until someone else volunteered the information that he was no longer there.

Only one person should speak at a time, and that person should move close to the phone. Speakers must identify themselves every time they speak because the distortion makes voice recognition difficult or impossible. If someone has to leave, he should say so and excuse himself.

Just the Fax, Please

The rules for using the fax machine are simple. The transmission should be expected, important, and specifically addressed to the person and the company. The cover sheet should give the date, the number of pages, the identities of the sender and the intended receiver, and the fax and regular phone numbers of both sender and receiver.

Be sure the original copy is clear because some fax printouts have distortions.

Netiquette

This word, borrowed from author Virginia Shea, refers to civil behavior on the Internet, but we will extend it to cover all aspects of communication by computer.

One reason that people create an unfavorable first impression when communicating by computer is a tendency to be playful and casual. They see their wonderfully resourceful computer as a novel gadget, full of ingenious elements and capable of wonderful tricks. This creates a dangerous tendency to treat it as a toy.

In addition to e-mail, chat rooms, and other forms of generally anonymous communications, many company systems allow employees to communicate with each other through the computer terminals at their desks. The style of these messages is generally informal, but you must resist the temptation to chat or, worse, gossip. A flip, off-color, or disparaging remark in an electronic message to a co-worker can be just as damaging to your reputation as if you had taken out a newspaper ad.

Netwits

As with every other aspect of communications, the people you deal with in cyberspace are judging you. They don't know what you look like, what you are wearing, or what your net worth is. All they can go by are your words. Choose them carefully. Being sloppy is insulting. Be careful about spelling and grammar, and don't ramble.

Don't be so sure that what you put out on the Internet is completely and forever untraceable. Law enforcement agencies have demonstrated recently that e-mail messages, for one thing, can be traced to their source. But even if all Internet messages were utterly untraceable, there are still very good reasons to be cyber-civil.

To begin with, we create messages in order to communicate. If your method is vulgar, obscure, or insulting, your message will not get through to most people. And, remember, those are *people* out there. You are looking at a screen, but the screen you see is much more than that. It is, in effect, a doorway. Be careful about the impression you make when you pass through that doorway.

And the screen doesn't scowl or smile or give any other hint as to how your words are being received. You have to rely on your good sense and sense of responsibility.

A good rule is never to write something on-line that you would not say in person. In other words, imagine yourself saying the words face-to-face with another person; if you wouldn't do that, try rewriting. Chances are you will find a way of expressing the same idea just as strongly and with a lot more effect.

Also, if you have a problem with someone on-line, think about how you would handle the situation in real life, and that will help you in resolving cyberstrife.

Bandwidth Bandits

When you send out e-mail or post something to a discussion group, you're taking up people's time (or at least hoping to).

In addition to wasting time, you are also taking up bandwidth. Only so much information can be transmitted at one time, and it has to be stored somewhere. When you (accidentally or otherwise) post the same note to the same newsgroup five times, you are wasting both time and bandwidth with electronic junk mail. This does not leave a good impression. Use e-mail responsibly.

Tips

Here are a few random rules of Internet politeness:

- Don't shout (which is done by writing in CAPITALS). For emphasis, use asterisks, like *this*.
- You don't have to begin with that "Dear Sir," "Dear Madam" business, but it's polite to sign your messages.
- Newbies (newcomers) should consult the lists of FAQs (frequently asked questions) before entering a newsletter group.
- Use the electronic equivalent of a polite cough, PMFJI (pardon me for joining in) before joining a group discussion.

The most effective way of presenting yourself in a favorable light while communicating electronically—either over the telephone line or through cyberspace—is to act as if the other person were standing right in front of you. Remember that people are no less apt to be offended, bored, annoyed, or pleased and grateful in response to your behavior just because they are in another room or on the other side of the world.

13

Compliments, Criticism, and Conflict

"**H**ello. I just wanted to say I thought your talk was pretty good. Sort of like one I heard last year in Memphis."

"Oh, thanks. It was kind of long, but I had a lot to cover."

Above is an example of two people making rotten first impressions on one another by simply ignoring the basic rules of giving and receiving compliments.

Some people may get their first impression of you when you are in situations involving conflict, when you are giving or receiving compliments, or when you are giving or receiving criticism. The mistakes made in handling yourself in these contexts almost invariably occur within the first few minutes, and these mistakes may be difficult or even impossible to remedy.

Even people that you have known for a while may get their first real impression of you—your character and your personality—watching you perform in these three areas. This is territory laced with landmines, no place to be wandering around without some mental terrain maps.

Let's start with the most pleasant of the three Cs—compliments.

Compliments

Giving

The crucial first few minutes here may be the time you take before actually complimenting someone. That's when you should take an honest look at *why* you are complimenting him or her.

The greatest danger here is the temptation to give a compliment because you think it will improve a relationship, call attention to yourself, or boost the morale of an employee. In fact, there is no reason on earth to give an insincere compliment. Few things are as transparent as a phony or forced compliment, and few things can wreck your credibility faster. If you don't mean it, don't say it.

If, for example, the presentation of a report is muddled and the substance lacked focus, don't compliment the person who gave the report. If you must say something, simply say thanks for making the report and change the subject. If, on the other hand, the report was good, don't damn it with faint praise. Be unqualified and specific: "I thought that was a fine report and well delivered. I was particularly impressed with your analysis of the regional dynamics and your assessment of insurance risks."

Don't make comparisons, unless you are prepared to compare an achievement with something truly outstanding, and this always sounds forced.

Remember that a compliment is a two-way street—it benefits the giver as well as the receiver. So don't hold back or put off congratulating or complimenting someone. It sounds lame to compliment people for something they did two weeks ago, unless you haven't seen them in the interim.

Also, do not neglect to say "Good job" simply because the person in question is consistently efficient and you don't want to sound repetitious. People like their efforts to be appreciated.

Receiving

Few things make a better first impression on people than the ability to receive a compliment with grace. And it's easy. When someone compliments you, just say "Thank you."

Some think they impress people as being modest if they try to shrug off a compliment. They don't. They impress people as being phony.

The phony modest response often takes the form of, "Oh, it was nothing." Well, if you think it was nothing, that means you think the person complimenting you must have pretty poor judgment. And, let's face it, you don't really want the other person to think your achievement was nothing, do you?

And, if you are complimented on doing a good job, don't say "It should have been more complete" or "It should

147

have been finished sooner." If someone compliments you on your appearance, don't say, "Oh, this old thing?" That implies that the other person has poor taste.

And never upgrade a compliment. If someone says your performance was good, don't say, "Good? It was terrific. Did you see the way I . . ."

If others deserve a share of the credit for whatever it is that brings a compliment, be sure to mention them.

Otherwise, please, just say "Thank you."

Criticism

Giving

Julia Gallagher shows up ready to make a presentation only to learn that there aren't enough chairs, there's no place to plug in the projector, and, worst of all, some of those attending got mixed messages about the date and time, causing last-minute confusion.

Afterward, she is introduced to Fred Antonio, who was in charge of organizing the meeting. She says, "Who taught you how to organize anything? You made a mess of this whole thing."

This remark is a sure winner, but only if Julia is aiming to get Fred to hate her, to diminish his effectiveness as a worker, and perhaps to spend the next several minutes engaging him in a tedious, possibly hostile, and certainly counterproductive conversation about what went wrong and who's to blame.

The first impression Julia is making on those around her, particularly those who don't know her, is worse than the first impression Fred made on her.

The purpose of criticism is to improve things, not to assign blame or to make yourself feel better. Fred's reaction to the negative comments will be to become defensive or cowed or angry, or all three.

When you must be critical:

- Don't criticize in public.

- Don't get personal. Don't call people names or say what they did was "dumb" or "wrong." Talk about behavior, not personality. "I think the presentation would have gone a lot better if you had spent more time on preparations."

- Be specific. It's not good enough to say the whole thing was a mess. "Next time, please double check the details, things like making sure that everybody shows on time and that the audiovisual equipment is plugged in and ready to go."

- Forget the sledgehammer. One way of criticizing without leaving a trail of blood is to begin with a compliment. "You're usually efficient, Fred. That's why I was so surprised at how badly things went today." This doesn't mean, however, that you should get into the habit of using the "but bomb" every time you want to deliver a criticism: "I like your report, but . . ."

- The "but bomb" tends to send people running for the air raid shelters. They know something negative is coming along to invalidate the first part of your remark, and they begin thinking of defenses. Better is: "I think your report lacked statistical backup. Next time, go heavier on the numbers."

Receiving

"Hey, I didn't know there was even going to be a presentation until this morning. And nobody said anything about audiovisual. It's not my fault if people didn't show up on time."

By this reaction, Fred is using the first minutes of his time with Julia Gallagher only to reinforce her negative impression of him. His first impulse on receiving criticism was to duck. Try to resist a similar impulse when you receive criticism.

If the criticism is justified, take it on the chin. Don't get defensive, try to switch the blame, whine, or grovel for forgiveness. Accept the situation as a problem that needs to be solved. Make it clear that you accept responsibility and that you want to fix the problem and/or make sure it doesn't recur: "I'm sorry for the foul-up. I can see now that you have to stay right on top of all of these details. I certainly will next time."

If the situation is personal: "I never intended to offend (embarrass, upset, trouble) you, but I can see that I have, and I'm sorry."

However, if you are getting a bum rap, it's a different story. If the criticism is unjustified, unnecessarily harsh, or delivered publicly, you have a perfect right to react.

But be cool. If you get angry and start returning fire, you are not going to make your point, and the situation could escalate so that you both say things you will regret later.

Usually, when feelings are running high, it's better to put off discussing things: "Let's talk about this when we're both a little calmer," or "We ought to get together and work this out. What's a good time for you?"

Criticism in the presence of others is always a bad idea. If it happens to you, one technique to end it is to try chilling the other person by stopping what you are doing or saying and then locking eyeballs with him for a moment before resuming. Or you can saying something like, "It's no good trying to hash this out in public. Tell me your problem (or objections) in private."

If you are not sure the criticism is justified and want some time to think about it, you can say:

"Thanks for letting me know what's on your mind, Kurt. I'd like to think it over and get back to you."

Handling Conflict Effectively

Except perhaps for Santa Claus, everybody encounters conflict. How you present yourself in conflict situations will do more for your reputation than a thousand-dollar suit.

Let's look at some conflict situations and possible reactions to them.

Ethnic Remarks

You are chatting with three co-workers, and one of them says, "He's a dumb Polack, which is worse than a dumb dago."

You have every right to be offended by this kind of talk, whoever you are, and you should not let it pass in the interest of office harmony. As soon as it happens, say, "That remark was out of line," or "If you feel that way, you should keep it to yourself."

If the other person wants to argue about it, don't cooperate. Walk away. You have made your point.

151

Sexual Harassment

Your reaction to any kind of sexual harassment has to be tough and immediate. Either deliver a two-fisted put-down on the spot, or go right to the senior officer in your company or to your department head, report the incident, and demand action.

If you decide on a put-down, try something like "What a stupid remark. Don't you know that you're making a fool of yourself?" Or, "I didn't realize how pathetic you are until this minute. You're really a silly little jerk."

If you decide to let the crumb off with a warning, make it a strong one: "I'm going to forget this happened, but if you ever do anything like it again, I'm going to raise so much hell around here that you'll never live it down."

Personal Attacks

Suppose you are in a group and someone attacks a friend of yours who is not present. You can't let it pass, and it's not good enough to say, "That's a lie."

It's downright counterproductive to go on the attack: "Look who's talking. You're the one who . . ."

Try something like, "I don't think that's the way it happened. Even if it is, I'm sure Alex had a good reason for reacting as he did."

If the other person asks what the reason could be, say, "I don't know. Why don't you ask Alex."

Offensive Jokes

Somebody starts telling what you are sure will be an off-color joke that will make you and perhaps others present uncomfortable. Just say, "I don't want to hear this," and move away. If you don't know the joke is going to be vulgar until it's too late, look the comedian right in the eye when he delivers the punch line, even if others have laughed at the joke, and say "I don't think that was the least bit funny."

Inappropriate Questions

"Are you two sleeping together?"

"How come you don't have any children?"

"How much do you make, anyway?"

Yes, people will ask stupid and insulting questions. If you don't want to come right out and tell them their questions are inappropriate, you can ignore them (which is a pretty good put-down), or you can look at them for a moment and say, "I'm not going to answer that." If you want to make them uncomfortable in front of others, you can say, "Why do you ask?"

Less insulting questions require lesser responses. If, for example, someone asks you how much your purse cost, and you don't want to answer, say "I don't remember."

Petitions

Suppose you are asked to sign a petition, and you don't agree with the position it takes. The last thing you want to do is get into an argument about the merits of the position, an argument that will change nobody's mind and may generate permanent hard feelings. You can say something like: "I've thought about this issue a lot, and

I'm afraid I can't support this petition. I hope you understand."

If the advocate persists, say "I'm sorry. That's the way I feel."

If you are not familiar with the issue, you could say, "I don't know enough about the issue right now to know whether I agree with the petition. I need some time to look into the matter."

Bad News Situations

There are situations in which the conflict will occur mostly within yourself: People get fired, go into bankruptcy, get indicted. You don't want to shun them, and you don't want to pretend nothing has happened, which puts both of you in the proverbial "elephant in the living room" situation. It's up to you to acknowledge the other person's misfortune and to offer your sympathy. Sure it's stressful, but it's a lot less stressful than the alternatives.

Tell the other person that you heard about what happened and that you're sorry. Ask if there is anything you can do, but only if you are truly willing to help out if called upon to do so.

Here is an example: You have worked with and spoken to Carla on an almost daily basis. You learn that she has received her termination notice. If she begins talking about the situation after you have expressed sympathy, be quiet and listen. You can nod to indicate you are listening, and when it is appropriate you can say something like: "This is really tough on you. I'm so sorry."

When discussing someone's bad news:

- Do not say you know of someone who is suffering even more. It's like telling a person who has a severe headache, "You should be glad you don't get migraines like my aunt Nellie."
- Do not join in criticism. If Carla wants to tell you that her boss is a Nazi scumbag, let her; but don't agree.
- Do not say that things will work out for the best.
- Do not offer unsolicited advice.
- Do not say, "I told you something like this would happen." In fact, don't indicate at all that the event was predictable or in any way the person's fault.
- Do use expressions such as:

  "I'm sorry you have to go through this."

  "It must be a great shock for you."

  "Is there anything I can do to help?"

First impressions are seldom more tied up with human feelings than in situations involving compliments, criticism, and conflict. It is helpful to remember the single theme that runs through all of the situations dealt with in this chapter. It's all about human dignity—a sense of your own worth and a respect for the dignity and feelings of others. This sense of self-worth will allow you to accept criticism without rancor and to deliver it without malice or meanness. It will allow you to bestow compliments generously and to accept compliments gracefully. It will let you deal with conflict in a way that does not diminish you or those with whom you are dealing.

14

Dining for Dollars

It was an emergency call, a rare occurrence in my business. On the line was the president of a hotel management firm in New York. One of his top managers was confronted with a table manners crisis.

The firm had recently been hired to manage an old-line luxury hotel in Charleston, South Carolina, the very capital of Southern gentility. The owners of the hotel had gotten a negative first impression of the manager sent down from New York to take over the operation. His table manners were unacceptable. This *was* Charleston, after all, and it simply would not *do*.

The next day, I met with the president, the CEO, and the manager for a crash course in table manners. It took the form of a seven-course dinner with wines in a private dining room at the Ritz Carlton in Philadelphia.

I was immediately impressed with the charm and intelligence of the manager. His only problem was that he hadn't learned some of the rules.

Making a good impression at the table requires common sense and a respect for the sensibilities of others, but it also requires a knowledge of certain rules. You can't expect to know these rules instinctively. You have to learn them. Everybody does. I did.

The manager returned to Charleston with new confidence, and there were no more complaints about his table manners. He called me later to say that he particularly enjoys observing the dining etiquette errors of his former critics—errors he is, of course, too polite to point out.

Tabletop Encounters

Every business executive knows that his first meeting with people he needs to impress may be at lunch or dinner. A good grounding in dining etiquette is crucial if he is to approach these meetings with confidence, sure that his behavior will not be a distraction or worse, an annoyance.

And this applies not only to those in the executive suite. Imagine that a prospective employer (or your fiancee's family) suggests that your first meeting be at a restaurant or that the company president invites you to a dinner party at his home.

We will start with a list of the most common and most serious mistakes people make while dining and then walk you through a business meal, which is—believe me—so much more than just a meeting with food. It is really a test that spotlights your social skills and your level of sophistication.

Common Errors

Some things to look out for:

- Holding your knife or your fork in your fist. Cutlery should be held in your fingers.

- Putting your cutlery back onto the table once it has been used. This includes resting the handles on the table, like oars of a rowboat. Lay them across the edge of your plate. (For more about cutlery, see "American vs. Continental Style" later in this chapter.)

- Chewing with your mouth open or speaking with food in your mouth. Keep your lips together until you have swallowed the food.

- Smoking, even in the smoking-permitted areas of restaurants, before the meal has ended. (Never, ever, use a plate as an ashtray. If you don't see an ashtray, don't smoke.)

- Slouching, squirming, or tilting your chair. Your mother was right. Sit up straight.

- Picking or poking at your teeth.

- Bad pacing—finishing a course before everyone else, or making everyone wait for you to catch up.

- Leaving lipstick smears.

- Buttering all of the bread at once. Tear off each bite-size piece, and butter it just before you eat it.

- Flapping your napkin to open it (simply unfold it), or putting the napkin on the table before the meal has ended. If you leave the table temporarily, leave the napkin on your chair.

- Putting purses, keys, gloves, and so on, on the table. Put them in your pocket or purse or on the floor.

There are, of course, other traps you can fall into, but you can avoid most of them by being attentive and considerate of the feelings of others at the table.

In addition to being careful about what you do, watch what you say. Don't complain about the food or the service. Don't talk about your health, good or bad. If someone leaves the table, don't ask where they are going. If someone takes a pill, don't ask what it's for.

Don't dunk anything or blow on a liquid to cool it. Cut only enough food for the next mouthful. Don't salt or season food before you taste it, and not even then if you think it might offend the host/chef. Don't push your chair away from the table when you have finished eating.

Handling Food Calamities

We must recognize the fact that accidents will happen. Try to respond to them as coolly as possible.

- If you spill something, don't dramatize the accident by jumping up or yelling. Blot with your napkin and ask the server for another one. If the napkin will not stem a flow coming toward you, move your chair back a bit.

- If you spill something on someone else, apologize and offer to pay for whatever dry cleaning might be needed. Do not touch the other person. Let the victim handle the wiping and blotting, although you should offer your napkin and ask the server for replacements.

- If you burp, touch your napkin to your lips and say, "Pardon me" to no one in particular.

American Style vs. Continental Style

Both the American and the Continental methods of handling cutlery are correct. The Continental style is more efficient and more commonly used outside the United States.

In the American style, the knife is used only for cutting. It is held in the right hand. The fork in the left hand is used to hold what is being cut. The knife is then placed on the edge of the plate, blade facing in, and the fork is switched to the right hand to pick up what has been cut. The hand not being used is in the lap.

With the Continental style, the knife remains in the right hand and the fork in the left. When the food is cut, the knife is used to push it onto the fork. The tines of the fork face down when the food is conveyed to the mouth. Some foods such as peas, must, of course, be conveyed with the tines facing up. The hands remain above the table from the wrist up when not being used.

The Business Meal

For this demonstration meal, you will be the host. Knowing what the host is doing and why he is doing it will help you to be a more confident and knowledgeable guest.

As host, it is your responsibility to make sure the items on your agenda for the meeting are accomplished. This means having things go as smoothly as possible so that there will be few distractions to divert attention from the focus of the meeting.

Except for celebrations, extravagance is bad manners and bad strategy. Stay away from expensive, ostentatious restaurants, and don't try to impress people by ordering the most expensive wines and dishes on the menu. You are apt to convey the message that you are reckless with money and, thus, possibly reckless in other areas.

The Location

Become familiar with a few good, reliable restaurants and their menus. So when the time comes, you can select a restaurant you know and trust (this is no time to try a new place). Become known as a "regular." Get to know the maitre d' or manager.

Visit the restaurant a day or two before the meeting. Find a table in a good position, and reserve it if possible. Introduce yourself to the manager or maitre d', and set up a corporate account or allow him to take a credit card imprint. Let him know if you will be ordering wine, state your price range, and ask for recommendations. This might be a good time to pretip the maitre d' or manager, usually $10 or $20, depending on the level of the restaurant.

Make it clear that this is an important business meal, that you are willing to pay for service, and that you and your associates will be returning to the restaurant regularly if all goes well.

Extending Invitations to Meals

This can be a situation that should be handled with care.

"Hello, Michael Fritz? This is Greg Phillips from Design Plus. We'll be consulting on the Gibson project. I'm calling to invite you to lunch to discuss some ideas for getting started. How does that sound?"

"Sounds good," Michael replies.

"You haven't met Elizabeth Yan or Paul Mullen from our marketing department, and I'd like to bring them along."

"That would be fine with me."

"How about Monday or Tuesday?"

"Monday's better."

"Good. How does the Palm or Alberto's sound to you?"

"Either one. Alberto's is probably quieter, though."

"I agree. Would twelve-thirty or one be more convenient?"

"Twelve-thirty."

"Smoking or nonsmoking?"

"Nonsmoking."

"Great. See you Monday at twelve-thirty at Alberto's."

Thus, you have established the purpose of the meeting, those attending, and the day, the time, and the place.

Confirming the Meeting

If it's a lunch or dinner meeting, call your guests to confirm on the morning of the meeting. If it's breakfast, confirm the afternoon before, and give your guests your home phone number in case they have an emergency. If the meeting is postponed for any reason, call the restaurant right away. The easiest way to earn a reputation as persona non grata in the restaurant community is to be a "no show."

Arriving for the Meal

As the host, you should be there ten or fifteen minutes early and check your coat. If you did not tip the maitre d' during your first visit, do so now, reminding him how many guests you are expecting. Wait near the door for your guests if possible. If you must wait at the table, leave your napkin on the table and do not eat or drink anything—in other words, the table setting should be undisturbed. Stand up when your guests arrive and remain standing until they are seated. If someone at the table excuses himself during the meal, it is not necessary for the host (or anyone else) to stand.

Arrange to sit at right angles with your principal guest, in this case, Michael. If convenient, he should be at your left, if you are right-handed. If there are two principal guests, try to avoid sitting between them or you will be doing the tennis match head-swivel throughout the meal. It's better to seat both on one side of you or sit opposite both.

Handling Napkins

Your napkin will be on the plate or to the left of it. Unfold it on your lap when you sit. If it's one of those extra large, dinner-size napkins, leave it half-folded. Never tuck it in your belt or shirt. If you leave the table, place the napkin on the chair and push the chair under the table. Keep the soiled part off the upholstery.

What'll You Have?

When the server asks if you want anything from the bar, decline if your guests do. If drinks are ordered, you can order something nonalcoholic if you wish. No explanations are necessary. You can remove any suggestion of judgment about alcohol by saying something like, "I'm not having wine today, but please do have some if you like." The "today" is the key word.

If no drinks are ordered, spend a few minutes in small talk before ordering the meal. If there are drinks, the server will return to ask about refills. If the answer is no, ask for the menus then. If the answer is yes, ask for menus when the second round arrives.

Ordering with Ease

This is where your previous exploration of the menu pays off. Give your guests clues about your intentions by mentioning specialities and encouraging them to order appetizers. Have the server take the guests' orders first and order the same number of courses yourself, whether you want them or not.

(As a guest, you should feel free to ask the host if he has any recommendations if he has not given any clues.)

This is no time for indecisiveness. Nobody should spend a long time studying the menu. Stay away from user-unfriendly items such as large sandwiches, spaghetti, or anything else that will be messy or difficult to eat.

Handling Bad Service

It is the host's responsibility to see that the guests are served properly. If you suspect that there is something wrong or missing, ask your guest. If there is a specific problem, summon the maitre d' and ask him to fix it.

If things are going badly in general, do not get into a confrontational situation with the server or maitre d' in front of your guests. Tell your guests, "I'm sorry. They seem to be having a bad day," and deal with the manager later. It's fine to excuse yourself and let the manager know there's a problem, asking that a different server be assigned.

Finishing the Meal

Encourage everyone to have dessert, and again follow their lead. Ask if they would like coffee or tea. When it is served, ask for the check. This is the right time to review your previous business discussions. Make sure everyone understands what agreements have been reached and what subsequent steps need to be taken.

Paying Up

It's fine to review the bill for accuracy. You should have a pretty fair idea of the total even before it arrives. Don't study the thing like a crucial contract, and never, ever, pull out your pocket calculator at the table. If you think there is a discrepancy, deal with it after your guests have left. Pay with a credit card or with a large bill if you are using cash.

Haggling over who should pay the bill can ruin the effect of a smooth business meal. Of course, there should be no question that the person doing the inviting does the paying.

However, haggling situations do arise. Unfortunately, this happens most often when a woman is the host, even in what we like to think of as our enlightened era. If the subject arises, depersonalize it by saying something like, "I invited you, and besides, ABC company would like to take you to lunch."

If you suspect that this sort of situation could arise, you can arrange beforehand to leave a credit card imprint with the provision for the addition of a tip of 18 or 20 percent. In this way, no check need be presented at the table.

Before you leave the table, collect the check room tickets from your guests so that you can tip that attendant $1 per garment on the way out.

Taking Leave

Escort your guests to the door. Shake hands and thank them for joining you. You can remind them about the next meeting or tell them that you will call them within a week to set up another meeting if one is needed.

Guests should thank the host, and if warranted they should praise the restaurant. Guests should also send a handwritten thank you note within two days. And, no, you can't get by with a telephone call, or worse, a fax or an e-mail thank you.

Eating on the Job

The basic rules for dealing with food ordered in for a meeting are to keep it simple and to keep it tidy.

Use a knife and fork if they are provided, but don't worry about using your fingers for foods like sandwiches, pizza, or chicken nuggets. If all you have to work with are those flimsy plastic knives and forks, you may find it more convenient to use your hands.

Keep the playing field clean. Stack those plastic ketchup wrappers instead of scattering them around. Use plenty of napkins, or better still, packaged moist towelettes, but be as unobtrusive about it as possible.

Bones and scraps go on the side of your plate, not on the table. Keep your place free of keys, your purse, or anything else not related to the food or the work (they should be in your pocket or purse or on the floor).

The Banquet

It's one of those nights of the round table—an awards banquet, a wedding reception, or the kickoff dinner of a week-long conference in the ballroom of the Grand Hotel. The room is a sea of linen, silverware, dishes, glassware, and candles. There are dozens of large round tables that are too close together and not nearly big enough for all of those dishes and glasses and cutlery, not to mention ten dressed-up people, some of whom you will be meeting for the first time.

You will be expected to keep your poise amid all of this confusion, and it can be a daunting proposition. Your only salvation is to handle it one step at a time.

Seating

To begin with, find your table and the place card with your name on it. *Do not* move place cards so you can sit next to your old pal Gus. Somebody went to a lot of trouble deciding on the seating arrangement, maybe even somebody who will be sharing your table. (This is an even more egregious breach of etiquette on smaller social occasions, when the host or hostess will not be happy about a guest fiddling with the carefully plotted seating arrangements.)

Before you sit down, take the opportunity to make a positive impression on your fellow diners by walking up to them, saying hello, and shaking hands. They will appreciate it, and it's a whole lot better than shouting your name across the table later on to people who, if they can hear it, probably won't remember it.

When it is time to sit down, *men*, it is neither sexist nor theatrical for you to hold the chair for the woman on your right. If it seems appropriate, do so. *Women*, accept the gesture with grace, but don't wait for it if it doesn't seem to be forthcoming.

The (Oh, No) Place Setting

Yes, all of that silver and glassware can be daunting. But try thinking of it as a chart that will guide you safely through unknown waters.

Look at the silverware. You will be using the cutlery *starting from the outside and working in*. Generally, you can predict the number of courses by looking at the silverware. (However, at a formal dinner, the server might replace silverware before each course.)

There might be so much stuff on the table that your principal concern is determining what belongs to you. Here's how to tell:

- Knives and spoons are on your right.
- All forks and napkins are on your left.
- Glasses for liquids are on your right. (A memory crutch is that "drinks" begins with DR—drinks right.)

- Plates for solid foods, such as salad and bread, are on your left.

If someone not as clued-in as you are takes over your bread plate, don't retaliate by using someone else's. Put your bread on the rim of your dinner plate.

Basic Table Courtesies

Once you have recognized what is yours, the rest is easy. Simply wait for the courses to come and go. However, because of the crowded conditions, some basic table courtesies become even more important:

- Keep your things, including your elbows and your napkin, off the table. If you are encumbered by objects, put them beside or under your chair. If you don't know what to do with your hands, put them in your lap.
- Once you have picked up a piece of silverware, it never touches the tabletop again. Utensils should be placed entirely on the plate, not tipped with part on the plate and part on the tabletop. The blade of the knife always faces you.
- The coffee-tea spoon (which you will find above the diner plate in some table settings) goes on the saucer beside the cup.

The Buffet

A buffet's an occasion when many ordinarily sensible people can foul up royally. Something primal seems to happen to them. They feel that somehow the food will be taken away before they get some, or that other people will take all of it, leaving them to starve. The result can be something resembling a fire drill in an ant hill, with people bumping into each other, reaching around and between others, and overloading their plates.

A Cautious Beginning

Check out the situation before you even approach the buffet table. Are the utensils and the plates on the buffet table or on the dining tables? Are there place cards on the dining tables? See if there are to be one or two lines at the buffet table. If there are two, there should be utensils on both sides.

Take your place in line. There are no gender preferences in lining up, but don't break up a couple or a group going through the line together.

Serving Yourself

Rule number one: Don't overload your dish. It is perfectly acceptable to go back for seconds and thirds. You may want to have soup or some salad first, go back for an entree and then for dessert or fruit.

Don't bring back food "for the table." Let others make their own decisions.

If an item is in short supply, go easy, or pass it up. At a hotel or restaurant it is okay to ask servers to replenish a dish, but never at a private party.

Use the serving spoon or fork intended for each particular dish, leaving it beside, and not in, the dish. A spoon left in a dish can become so hot that it could burn people's fingers.

At a serving station, don't ask the attendant for something he cannot easily do. For example, don't ask for "over easy" at the omelet station if you can see there are no whole eggs in sight. And don't ask for omelet ingredients if you can see that they are not readily available. Don't ask for end cuts of beef if you can see that there are none left.

Handling Plates

In a restaurant or a hotel, you shouldn't have to reuse a plate or utensils. If replacements are not readily available, ask a server to replenish the supply. At a private party, use common sense in deciding whether to reuse your plate. In any case, never scrape and stack plates. That kind of helpful housecleaning is out of place and generally not appreciated.

Sitting, Standing

If you have been assigned a seat, sit in it. If not, and if people invite you to join them as you leave the buffet line, accept graciously, or say "Thanks, but I promised Laura and her family I'd eat with them." People will be coming and going at different times, so don't stand up for every new arrival. If you leave the table, put your napkin on your chair. Fold it in such a way that nothing on the napkin could stain the upholstery.

If you will be eating standing up, as at a cocktail party, it is even more important that you not overload your plate.

Take up a position that does not block access to the buffet table or anything else.

While it is important to know and observe the rules of table manners, it is also important to remember that sharing food with others can be one of the most pleasant aspects of life. Approach these occasions with the expectation that they will be pleasant. And remember that at mealtime, the best sauce is conversation.

15

A World of Diversity

Terry Newman arrives for a meeting with a senior executive of a major Asian corporation that he hopes will end up buying a lot of machine parts from his company. Terry is psyched for the meeting, during which he wants to establish a good working relationship. He is kept waiting fifteen minutes, which is annoying, but he is not going to let that get in the way of his determination to impress this executive with the fact that he is a friendly guy.

Terry strides into the office, approaches the other man, sticks out his hand, makes eye contact, smiles, and says, "I'm pleased to meet you." He immediately sits down in the chair in front of the desk, props his left ankle on his right knee to show how relaxed and friendly he is, and says, "I'm really glad to have this opportunity to present our line of products and to make some suggestions as to how they can fit into your production scheme. Let me start by going over the basics."

While he is talking, Terry notices that the emotional temperature in the room has gone down about twenty degrees. The ensuing conversation is brief and vague and ends with a statement that perhaps someone might be calling Terry at some unspecified future time. He leaves feeling as if he has been to the principal's office.

Different Folks

Terry has a lot to learn. The standard way in which Americans greet one another will not go over well everywhere in our expanding global economy. In fact, it can be inappropriate right here at home, where cultural diversity is richer than ever. For example, more than 31 million people in the United States now speak English as their *second* language.

For many of us, our first instinct when greeting someone is to put out our hand, make eye contact, and smile. In some situations, this could be making three mistakes all at once.

Hands Across Cultures

When meeting Asians for the first time, it is a good idea not to be the one to initiate the handshake. You could be forcing the kind of physical contact with which the other person is uncomfortable. Of course, many Asians have learned to accept the handshake when dealing with Westerners. Still, let them make the offer to shake hands. When shaking hands with a Japanese person, it is polite to accompany the gesture with a slight bow of the head because the bow is the customary greeting in Japan. But don't make a big deal out of it. Westerners are not expected to be familiar with the complexities of Japanese bowing protocol.

Shaking hands is now an accepted form of greeting in most Western and Middle Eastern cultures.

A Smile's Meaning

In North America and in many other parts of the world, the smile is a harmless expression of friendliness. Its meaning is unambiguous for us. It means someone is happy or amused or sending out a friendly signal.

However, in some Asian cultures, smiling is considered a gesture best reserved for informal occasions, and smiling during a formal introduction can be considered disrespectful or at least frivolous. And in some Latin cultures, a smile may be used to say "Excuse me" or "Please."

Westerners, however, are pretty much at liberty to smile when greeting people anywhere. If someone does not return your greeting smile, however, it does not necessarily indicate aloofness or hostility.

Making Eye Contact

It is a sign of respect in many cultures to deliberately avoid eye contact. In some places, "look 'em right in the eye" is considered downright belligerent. For example, there have been cases in which hostility has broken out between customers and Korean shopkeepers in American cities. The Koreans avoid eye contact as a gesture of respect, and the customers interpret that as a insult. Also, some American teachers have said that at first they thought Asian students were not paying attention because they did not look at the teacher while he or she was speaking. So, if people from another culture seem to be avoiding eye contact with you, don't worry. They are probably just being polite.

Physical Contact

Most Latins are accustomed to physical contact, and people who know each other only slightly may embrace when greeting one another. Middle Easterners, particularly Muslims, avoid physical contact with people of the opposite sex. However, people of the same sex often hug each other when greeting. Also, a short, crisp handshake may be offensive to Middle Easterners, and people should be careful not to pull their hand away too quickly.

Many Asians are touchy about touching. For example, don't take hold of the arm of a Japanese during a conversation, much less drape your arm over his shoulder. And don't be offended if an Asian shopkeeper places your change on the counter instead of in your hand. He is just being polite.

Men holding hands, seen by some Americans as a signal of a homosexual relationship, is a common gesture of friendship in some countries, particularly in the Mediterranean and in the Middle East.

Dumping Stereotypes

If you are going to be dealing with people from around the world, you may be carrying some attitudinal baggage that needs to be jettisoned immediately. Despite the gems of conventional wisdom:

- Asians are not necessarily remote and "inscrutable."

- Not all Latin cultures hold the siesta inviolate.
- Germans are not all cold and hyperefficient.
- Japanese are not basically shy.
- Visitors from overseas are not always delighted to be taken to ethnic restaurants serving what we might consider to be their favorite foods.
- Gestures and hand-waving, accompanied by English words spoken loudly, will not bridge the language gap. Noise never helps, of course, and as we will see, certain gestures can be downright insulting.

Making a Gesture

Americans point to their chests to indicate "me." The Chinese point to their noses.

In Colombia, people tap their elbows with their fingertips to say that someone is stingy.

Terry Newman committed a gross violation of etiquette when he sat in a position that exposed the sole of his shoe to his host. In most Asian countries and in parts of the Middle East, this is considered a deliberate and vulgar insult.

Familiar and seemingly innocent gestures can get you into trouble while traveling abroad. These include pointing with the index finger, giving the thumps-up sign, or making a circle with the thumb and the index finger.

In some countries, you will see people clap their hands or snap their fingers to summon waiters or servants. However, it is wise for the visitor to avoid doing either. Also, avoid using the crooked index finger in a beckoning gesture.

179

The "V for victory" sign or the sign for "two" of something, is insulting in England and Ireland if the palm is turned inward. In fact, this is another gesture that should be avoided altogether.

In some cultures, it is considered rude to engage in conversation with your arms akimbo or folded over your chest.

Spaced Out

In dealing with people from other cultures, it is important not to engage in space wars.

Westerners are accustomed to standing about eighteen inches from each other when conversing. If the distance between the two conversing is greater, one of them will generally move closer. If the distance is less, one or both may back up.

Asians stand farther away during conversation, and Latins and many Mediterraneans stand closer than some of us are used to. Inexperienced North Americans, if they feel crowded, will back off. This often doesn't work because the other person will simply advance, and you could end up being backed up against a wall. In situations such as this, I have found it helps to turn slightly away from the face-to-face position instead of backing up. On the other hand, if the person with whom you are speaking moves back, resist the urge to pursue him.

Dining Diversity

Some of us would sooner eat a rat's tail than a cooked snail. And those who consider snails a delicacy can't imagine how anyone could willingly eat corn on the cob or pumpkin pie.

We Westerners have to acknowledge that others may find our eating habits disconcerting. We do business over breakfast, and lunch is little more than an afterthought. We indulge in an odd practice called "brunch." We load our water glass with ice and drink denatured (decaffeinated) coffee and cold tea.

In many countries, the main meal is taken at midday. In the United States it comes at the end of the work day, usually within an hour, either way, of 7 P.M. Elsewhere a minor meal is served in the evening, usually later. In Spain, supper sometimes begins around 10 P.M.

This is a good place to explain English "tea." This is a light meal taken around 4 P.M. and consisting generally of tea, small sandwiches, and pastries. "High tea" is not a more elaborate version of "tea," but an informal replacement for supper.

Handling "Strangeness"

Tolerance and an open mind are necessary when it comes to what is and what is not strange when it comes to the subject of food.

Some people in Japan eat horse meat. Sea urchins are popular in Korea, sea slugs in China, sheep eyes in the Middle East, kidney pie in England, and a mixture of sheep's organs and entrails called "haggis" in Scotland.

And some foreigners have trouble understanding how Americans can eat sweet potatoes, grits, hot dogs, or marshmallows. Many Europeans consider corn on the cob fit only for animals.

Also, Americans tend to have inaccurate ideas about foreign cuisine. What some consider to be Mexican or Chinese food would not be welcome in Mexico or China.

Don't despair, however. There are some general rules of etiquette that will help you get though culinary crises.

- If you are served an unfamiliar dish, you may be happier not asking what it is. Taste it. If you don't like it, cut it up and move it around on your dish so that it looks as if you are eating it. If the host asks your opinion, say, "It has a very distinctive flavor. I've never had anything like it." And smile.

- If you know what it is and don't want to eat it, refuse politely. If you are worried about offending your host, say something like: "I know this is a delicacy, but I've tried it before, and I find it doesn't sit well with me."

Culinary Caveats

Some things to look out for:

- Hosts should know that it is particularly important to respect the dietary laws of others. For example, vegetarianism is much more widespread than ever before. Muslims do not eat the flesh of any animal that scavenges, such as pigs, goats, and some birds. Muslims do not drink alcohol or eat foods cooked with alcohol. Many Jews do not eat pork or shellfish. Meat and fowl must be kosher, which means it must have been slaughtered, prepared, and cooked in compliance with Jewish law. Meat and dairy products are not served together.

- In Europe, the main dish is often served before the salad. If you are invited to a Chinese banquet, remember that these consist of many courses, so you should eat sparingly at the beginning. Do not point with your chopsticks, and don't stick your chopsticks upright in your rice bowl. It is considered to be bad luck.

Doing Business

When asked about their problems in dealing with business people from the United States and Canada, foreign executives generally cite three examples:

1. Our famous friendliness too often turns out to be shallow and short-lived. It falsely implies the possibility of an ongoing friendship or personal relationship. Some relationships call for a more restrained and formal approach than you may be accustomed to.

2. Our "let's get right down to business" attitude is disconcerting to many, as is the "work hard, play hard" attitude implied in the working breakfast and stand-up lunch. In some situations, it's best to approach business issues less directly.

3. We tend to believe that everyone enjoys being called by his or her first name by those who were strangers

two minutes ago. Generally, it's best not to use first names unless a person asks you to.

Problems with Gifts

Giving and receiving gifts is another area in which cultural diversity tends to produce a landscape full of antipersonnel mines.

For example, if you effusively admire a possession of another person, particularly if you are a guest, that person may feel compelled to offer the object to you as a gift. You, however, must firmly but politely refuse.

Even so innocent a gift as flowers can be misinterpreted. White flowers symbolize mourning among Chinese, and yellow flowers have similar negative connotations among Latins and Middle Easterners. In Europe, red roses often signal romantic intentions, and chrysanthemums are linked with death.

Here are some other things to keep in mind:

- In some Asian cultures, including Japanese and Chinese, gifts are not opened in the presence of the donor.

- In the Middle East, do not give gifts that are representations of partially clad women, or of animals, even pets, which are considered to be lowly creatures.

- Clocks are considered inappropriate gifts among Chinese, and cash gifts to Chinese should be in even numbers and should be given with both hands.

- A handkerchief suggests tears or parting in the Middle East.
- Gifts of knives can be considered symbolic of "cutting" a relationship in some Latin cultures.
- In Korea, the name of a living person is never written in red.

High Context, Low Context

Anthropologist Edward T. Hall's concept of "high-context, low-context cultures" provides some insights that can help us avoid problems when dealing with those from other cultures.

In low-context cultures, such as in the United States, Canada, Western Europe, and Scandinavia, it is considered virtuous to deal with unambiguous messages, lots of specificity, and crystal clear descriptions. Time is a linear proposition, and a straight line is the best way to get from point A to point B.

The road from point A to point B in high-context cultures—China, Japan, Korea, Spain, Greece, Turkey, Latin America, and the Arab world—has lots of curves and detours and scenery.

Low-context people tend to view high-context people as mysterious—inscrutable at best and sneaky and secretive at worst.

High-context people think low-context people move too fast and are insensitive, gabby, pushy, and redundant.

So it's important for Americans to recognize that they are low-context people and that they will have to make

---

some adjustments if they wish to move comfortably in high-context societies.

Let's say our friend Terry Newman has been clued in to all of this and is prepared to do a better job of handling a meeting with an executive from a high-context culture.

Terry arrives for the meeting promptly at the designated time of 2 P.M., even though he expects to be kept waiting. His expectation is fulfilled. He waits quietly, without reading or otherwise busying himself in a way that would indicate that the upcoming meeting is not his main reason for being there.

The host comes out to greet him and offers to shake hands. Terry shakes, bowing his head slightly. When they enter the office, he is not surprised to find others present. He greets everyone individually, with more handshakes, again offered by the others first. He does not sit down until his host indicates where he should sit and not until his host is seated. He keeps both feet on the floor.

If refreshments are offered, he accepts only after a mild and insincere refusal. He uses his right hand to drink, as is customary. Pleasantries are exchanged. Terry doesn't bring up the reason for his visit until the host has indicated that the time has come.

All the while, lots of things are happening around him. There are a number of conversations being held on and off, and there are telephone calls. The host may digress from the main topic often, but he will always come back to it.

Ultimately, opinions and positions will become known, business will get done, and Terry will be ushered out cordially.

The process may seem inefficient and may take a lot longer than Terry might consider necessary, but it works just fine for a considerable portion of the world.

∷

The world is a complex mosaic of customs and attitudes, and even the most well-intentioned, well-informed pilgrim is bound to stumble along the way.

Although it is not possible to always be "correct," a willingness to confess ignorance and ask for help, the ability to apologize sincerely and gracefully, and a friendly, open attitude will make up for most behavioral sins.

And don't let worry about possible social blunders make your relations with people of other cultures overly stiff or mannered. Approach learning about new people and cultures with a spirit of adventure and a genuine desire to learn, and you will not go too far wrong.

16

The Disabled in the Workplace

Gail Spenser rolls her wheelchair out of the elevator and up to the receptionist's desk: "Good morning. I'm Gail Spenser, here to see Margaret Hamilton."

The receptionist's mouth drops open: "Oh, I didn't know you were. . . . I mean, I'll tell her." The receptionist recovers from her shock only to become solicitous: "Can I get you anything? A pillow?"

Spenser, with considerable effort, manages to smile: "No, thank you."

When Hamilton buzzes and tells the receptionist she will see Ms. Spenser, the receptionist comes around the desk and takes hold of the wheelchair handles.

"I'll manage, thanks," Spenser says. "Just direct me to Ms. Hamilton's office."

The receptionist returns to her desk with the uncomfortable feeling of having done something wrong without knowing exactly what.

Overcoming Awkwardness

Even the most self-possessed people have a tendency to become socially disabled when they meet those with disabilities. They can become hesitant, uncomfortable, and unsure of themselves.

Part of this may have something to do with being reminded of our own vulnerability, but mostly, it has to do with not knowing how to behave toward those with disabilities.

But you can expect to encounter people with disabilities in all walks of life. There are, after all, 43 million people in the United States with disabilities, and it has become easier for them to join in the mainstream of life, particularly in the workplace, since passage of the Americans with Disabilities Act.

It will be easier for you to put aside any discomfort you may feel when meeting disabled people if you remember that they want to put you at ease just as much as you want to put them at ease. Maybe more.

These encounters are tougher on them because they have to deal with physical difficulties and restrictions as well as concerns about establishing a relationship with people they have never met before.

The Three Rs

For your part, just think of the three Rs:

- *Respect.* Extend the same respect to those with disabilities as you would to anyone else.

- *Relax.* There is no real reason for you to be tense or anxious. Take it easy, and behave naturally.
- *Reason.* Common sense and common courtesy will help you avoid most mistakes and will help you to correct those you do make.

Some Helpful Tips

Let's go over some tips on how to avoid the most common and most irritating mistakes people make when dealing with the disabled:

- Always offer to shake hands, unless this is obviously beyond the ability of the other person.
- Don't shout.
- Don't forget that you are dealing with an adult. Don't patronize. Don't pat. Don't use first names until they tell you it is all right.
- Speak directly to the disabled person, and not through a third person. This is even more important when addressing a hearing-impaired person. If someone is signing for the person, resist the temptation to speak to the signer.
- If you offer assistance, wait until the offer is accepted. Listen to the form that the assistance should take, and do not go beyond that.
- Don't distract a working guide dog in any way.
- Think of a wheelchair as an extension of the user's body. Don't touch, lean on, or move a chair without permission.

Regular Conversation

Don't worry about using the common cliches of everyday life:

"Running around."

"See you later."

"Did you hear . . ."

Don't worry about topics. Disabled people have as wide a range of interests as anyone else, including politics, families, and hobbies. And, of course, there's always the job, the dumb boss, the weather, the hometown football team.

This doesn't mean the subject of their disability is taboo. If it comes up, talk about it. If you have a question, ask it: "The auditorium has a disabled entrance at the side. Shall we head for that?" or "The meeting is at noon. Shall I come by for you, or will you get there on your own?"

There are, however, some expressions it is wise to avoid. Use "disabled" instead of "handicapped." Some people object to the word *handicapped* because it derives from "cap in hand," a reference to begging. Say, "uses a wheelchair" instead of "wheelchair-bound."

Never say "cripple," "victim," "invalid" (which connotes not valid), "unfortunate," "pitiful," "dumb" (as in mute), or "deformed." Such terms are not only cruel but vulgar.

Wheelchair Etiquette

Once again, don't touch the wheelchair.

Don't help without asking. Good times to ask if help is needed is when there is a steep incline or heavy shag carpet to traverse.

If you can do so comfortably, get to eye level when holding a conversation. It is impossible to deal with someone as an equal if one of you is looking up and the other looking down.

Don't move a wheelchair or crutches out of reach of a disabled person. This can cause discomfort or even panic. If you are giving a party or social function, think about access and obstacles.

Relations with the Visually Impaired

Blind people generally like to do as much as they can on their own. But you should go ahead and offer assistance if you think it might be helpful.

Let's say you see a blind man without a guide dog stopped at an intersection. It may be that he is stopped because he is waiting for assistance. You ask him if he wants to go across with you. If he says no, don't insist. Otherwise, offer your elbow, not your arm. Contact with the elbow makes it much easier for the blind to sense direction shifts. You will then be walking a step ahead. The movement of your body will let him know if you change direction. Hesitate, but don't stop, at the curb. Say "Curb" or "Step up."

Don't touch or speak to a working dog. While in harness, they are trained to treat humans as objects to be avoided. Don't distract them. Even if a dog is out of harness, don't pet it without permission.

Don't move anything, even a magazine, in a blind person's accustomed environment. If you do, put it back exactly where you found it.

193

Give directions with the blind person as the reference point: "You are facing Main Street. Third Street is on your right, and Elm Street is one block to your left."

When helping someone into a car, place his hand on the inside door handle. When giving someone a seat, place his hand on the back of the chair.

Don't let a sense of protectiveness prevent you from telling a blind person his tie is crooked or she has egg on her lapel.

Be aware of your voice level. For some reason, people tend to raise their voice when speaking to a blind person.

Gabe Tolliver, a blind man, takes over the office next to yours. You go in to say hello. The first thing you do is to announce your presence. If others are with you, introduce them: "This is Pete Bunche on my left and Mary Gomes on my right."

You offer to shake hands, saying, "Allow me to shake your hand." If Gabe extends his hand first, take it or, if you can't, say why: "I'd like to shake your hand, but I'm afraid I'll drop these files."

You speak to Gabe in a normal tone of voice. Use people's names as a clue as to whom you are addressing. Use Gabe's name if you are expecting a reply from him. If Gabe has to sign a document, provide a guiding device such as a ruler or a card.

Excuse yourself when leaving. You don't want to walk out and leave Gabe talking to thin air.

194

Relations with Those with Hearing Loss

This is a less dramatic disability than blindness, but it is more common and comes in various degrees of severity.

If new colleague Gabe has a hearing instead of a visual impairment, there is a whole other set of considerations to keep in mind.

When you go into his office, it might be necessary to tap him on the shoulder or to wave to get his attention before you speak. You learn that shouting does not work. You speak slowly and clearly without exaggerated lip movements. However, people with hearing loss are apt to rely to some degree on expressions, gestures, and body language.

Some deaf people rely entirely on lipreading, and many people with partial hearing loss may depend on it to some degree. So, when speaking to Gabe, make sure you face him directly, preferably on the same eye level, and don't turn away until you have finished speaking. Keep your hands away from your face while speaking. If convenient, stand where the most light will be on your face.

If he doesn't understand what you are saying right way, don't keep repeating the same phrases. Be flexible. If "I'll bring Donna Forti by later" doesn't work, try, "Donna Forti and I will come to your office this afternoon."

You can bend down a little to get closer to Gabe's ear, if that helps, but don't speak directly into the ear. Shouting close to the ear can be damaging.

If there is a group present and people are laughing at something that Gabe has not caught, explain the joke to him, or signal that you will explain later.

195

Relations with Those with Speech Impairment

When you encounter people who have difficulty speaking, be prepared to give them your close and patient attention. Don't interrupt, finish sentences for them, or correct their pronunciation.

Where possible, ask questions that require brief answers or that can be answered with a nod or gesture. Don't pretend to understand if you do not. If there is any doubt, repeat what you thought you heard, and let the other person's reaction guide you.

Developmental Disabilities

Dealing with those with developmental disabilities or retardation—particularly in the workplace—could present you with the most difficulties. It is important for you to have some basic background information. Treat the developmentally disabled as normally as possible, and set the same standards for them as for others. If they behave inappropriately, be prepared to tell them so in a manner that is firm but not critical or harsh.

Do not allow them to become too affectionate, and be careful about touching them because that could signal that such behavior is appropriate.

Accept the fact that repetition will be necessary in training the developmentally disabled, and be prepared to be patient.

Often, these people are extra sensitive to body language and tone of voice. Make sure your approach is as non-threatening as possible. Be firm but pleasant, and use a friendly tone of voice. Criticism and accusations have a demoralizing effect on everyone and particularly on those with developmental disabilities. "Let's try it this way" or "How about doing it like this" is a lot better than "That's wrong" or "You made a mistake."

Difficult Adjustments

While we are discussing meeting with and relating to the disabled, we should say a word about those who have become disabled later in life. They often need special consideration.

If you have colleagues or friends who have lately become disabled, remember that one of their most common reactions is extreme self-consciousness and an acute sensitivity to pity reactions on the part of the able-bodied.

They have lost the ability to do some of the things that defined them in their own minds and that were crucial to their sense of self-worth. They may have lost their jobs or been given lesser roles in the workplace. All of this adds up to a loss of self-esteem, depression, and/or anger.

You can help by acknowledging that life now is a lot more difficult and complicated for them without making maudlin expressions of pity. You can be prepared to shrug off displays of bad temper and frustration—they are not directed at you personally.

Other factors in the lives of the lately disabled are boredom and a wish for structure. Get them involved in activities and projects if you can. Provide structure by making appointments and arrangements with very particular details, and stick to them.

■■

People with disabilities are like the rest of the people you meet every day, except that they have had to be a little tougher, a little braver, and a little more determined and resourceful.

If you are uncomfortable in their presence, it is your fault, not theirs. They don't want your pity, and they deserve your respect and admiration.

Index

About the Authors

Mary Mitchell is a graduate of the College of New Rochelle in New Rochelle, New York. She did graduate work in mass communications at the American University in Cairo, Egypt, she worked for several years in public relations, and in 1989, she founded Uncommon Courtesies, a firm specializing in training people from all walks of life to use social skills to improve their relationships with others. Having spent 15 years developing a national reputation for public relations and special events through her agency, the Mitchell Organization, Ms. Mitchell began to specialize in corporate etiquette.

Ms. Mitchell is the author of "Ms. Demeanor," a popular twice-weekly syndicated behavioral column for children in the *Philadelphia Inquirer.*

Deeply committed to the principle that learning good manners is not the privilege of the privileged, Ms. Mitchell plays an active volunteer role at the Gesu School, an inner-city elementary school in North Philadelphia.

Ms. Mitchell has written two previous books: *Dear Ms. Demeanor: The Young Person's Etiquette Guide* (Contemporary Books, 1994) and *The Complete Idiot's Guide to Etiquette* (Macmillan, 1966). She has appeared nationally on "Good Morning America," "Fox Style News," PBS, TBS, "Working Woman," and Lifetime. Her work has been featured in numerous national publications, including *The Wall Street Journal, McCall's, Reader's Digest, New Woman, Cosmopolitan, Prevention, Better Homes and Gardens, Parents,* and *Parenting.*

Ms. Mitchell has received several Pepperpot and Silver Anvil Awards from the Public Relations Society of America, a Neographics Award for design of collateral materials, and a Ford Foundation fellowship for writing. Having travelled extensively and lived in South America, Europe, and the Middle East, Ms. Mitchell brings to her work an international perspective on the cultures and customs of other lands.

An avid sculler with Bachelors Barge Club, the oldest rowing club in the United States, Ms. Mitchell is also a distance runner. She is married to Daniel Fleischmann, a restaurateur and accomplished martial artist. They live happily and peacefully in Philadelphia without pets or children.

John Corr is a columnist and feature writer for the *Philadelphia Inquirer*, where he has been a foreign correspondent, education writer, book reviewer and entertainment columnist. He currently writes a daily column dealing with politics and social commentary.

He has worked for a number of other newspapers, including the *Pretoria News* in South Africa, has been a Nieman Fellow in Journalism at Harvard University, and has taught journalism at the graduate and undergraduate levels.